First published 2002
Researched and written by Ronald Turnbull
Field checked and updated 2008 by Ronald Turnbull
Series Management: Bookwork Creative Associates
Series Editors: Sandy Draper and Marilynne Lanng
Series Design Concept: Elizabeth Baldin and Andrew Milne
Picture Research: Liz Stacey
Proofreader: Pamela Stagg
Cartography provided by the Mapping Services Department of AA Publishing

Produced by AA Publishing
© Automobile Association Developments Limited 2009

Published by AA Publishing (a trading name of Automobile Association Developments Limited,
whose registered office is Fanum House, Basing View, Basingstoke, Hampshire RG21 4EA;
registered number 1878835)

Enabled by | Ordnance Survey® This product includes mapping data licensed from the Ordnance
Survey® with the permission of the Controller of Her Majesty's
Stationery Office. © Crown Copyright 2009. All rights reserved. Licence number 100021153.

A03370

ISBN: 978-0-7495-5593-1

A CIP catalogue record for this book is available from the British Library.

The contents of this book are believed correct at the time of printing. Nevertheless, the
publishers cannot be held responsible for any errors or omissions or for changes in the
details given in this book or for the consequences of any reliance on the information it
provides. This does not affect your statutory rights. We have tried to ensure accuracy in this
book, but things do change and we would be grateful if readers would advise us of any
inaccuracies they may encounter.

We have taken all reasonable steps to ensure that these walks are safe and achievable by
walkers with a realistic level of fitness. However, all outdoor activities involve a degree of risk
and the publishers accept no responsibility for any injuries caused to readers whilst following
these walks. For more advice on walking safely see page 144. The mileage range shown on the
front cover is for guidance only – some walks may be less than or exceed these distances.

Visit AA Publishing's website www.aatravelshop.com

Colour reproduction by Keenes Group, Andover
Printed by Printer Trento Srl, Italy

Acknowledgements
The Automobile Association would like to thank the following photographers, companies and
picture libraries for their assistance in the preparation of this book.

3 AA/S Day; 9   AA/N Hicks;
82/3 britainor   3 AA/A
Lawson; 118/9

Every effort h   lvance for
any accidenta   g edition of
this publicatic

Right: Dunkery Beacon, Exmoor National Park (Walk 9)

50 WALKS IN

Somerset

50 WALKS OF 2–10 MILES

Contents

Contents

Rating

Each walk is rated for its relative difficulty compared to the other walks in this book. Walks marked +++ are likely to be shorter and easier with little total ascent. The hardest walks are marked +++

Walking in Safety

For advice and safety tips see page 144.

Locator Map

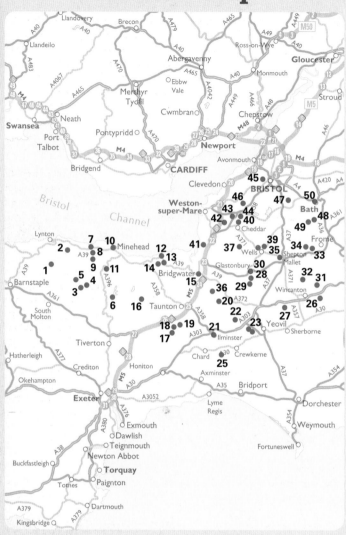

Legend

	Walk Route		Built-up Area
➊	Route Waypoint		Woodland Area
– – –	Adjoining Path	🚻	Toilet
☼	Viewpoint	🅿	Car Park
●	Place of Interest	🐙	Picnic Area
⌂	Steep Section	)(	Bridge

Introducing Somerset

In ancient Greek mythology, when Zeus sent two eagles to fly inwards from the ends of the Earth he discovered that the centre of everything was at the sacred oracle of Delphi. Today, in Somerset, he'd have to use buzzards. One bird would start at the Avon Gorge, soaring across the wide, traffic-noisy space below the Clifton Bridge; the other would rise out of an ancient oak by Badgworthy Water or, as it is better known, 'Doone Valley'. You don't need a ruler to work out that the two would meet at Glastonbury. Alighting on the top of Glastonbury Tor, they would look down on the town that stretches across time as effortlessly as our two birds stretch across space – from ancient through medieval to modern.

Gold Country

Somerset's towns of golden limestone, tile and thatch are the first part of what the county's all about. Looking outwards, our birds next observe the bumpy nature of the surroundings: Somerset may not be high, but it is hilly. In the far west a brown line along the horizon is the edge of Exmoor – more than half of the National Park is in our county, including its highest point at Dunkery Beacon. Slightly closer come the Brendons and the Blackdowns: rounded, friendly hills, criss-crossed with little lanes. To the south are the 'Green Hills of Somerset', famous enough to have their own song, and finished off on top with an Iron Age fort. Then there are the Mendips and the Quantocks: small but splendid limestone, covered with rabbit-nibbled meadow and wild flowers. Apologies here to Yorkshire: the finest limestone scenery, the best of the crags and gorges, is here among the Mendips. Closest of all are the tiny Poldens, their steep sides clothed with woodland and one proud outcrop of crag. By my count Somerset has seven hill ranges – that's one more than the whole of Snowdonia...

Admittedly Snowdonia's hills are bigger, but when you look out from Snowdon all you get is a narrow valley and another hill on the other side. Look out from a Somerset hill and you see a patchwork of bright fields. At sunset, from Glastonbury Tor, those fields have a green glow that's almost like dragon skin. Every few miles there rises another of Somerset's golden-orange church towers, and a silver river winds into the distance.

The Levels

These rivers bring us to Somerset's most special sort of country. Elsewhere in England there are flat lands – Lincolnshire, Norfolk, the Cambridgeshire Fens – and flat they certainly are, but only from the Somerset Levels do you look up to the hills; and from the hills you look down over the Levels. A typical Somerset walk might be a wander through the reclaimed wetlands, among butterflies and reed beds, followed by a hill that could be as tiny as Burrow Mump (100ft/30m) for a wide view back across it all. With hilltops at the top, and the Levels at the bottom, that still leaves the hillsides. Somerset hillsides are surprisingly steep –

PUBLIC TRANSPORT

Somerset has an efficient network of railways and bus routes. The steam-hauled West Somerset Railway (from Bishops Lydeard, near Taunton, to Minehead) and the Heart of Wessex Line from Bristol to Weymouth can be used to create fine cross-country walks. Bus timetables and maps are usually found in local libraries, as well as tourist information centres. Any one route may have multiple operators – check your proposed journey on the national travel phone line (0879 200 2233) or online (www.traveline.com).

there's a reason for this, involving the basically horizontal geology. They are also surprisingly green. Hillside woodlands, many of them of ancient oak or beech, grow dense and bushy. Thus another typical walk might follow a little stream, running up inside a big wood, and an open, airy hilltop above it all.

A Land of Riches

But then there are the stone-built towns to admire, the limestone gorges to marvel at, the legendary footprints of Kings Arthur and Alfred to retrace; there are the Doones to be done, and the literary walking of Samuel Taylor Coleridge; there's even some Somerset shoreline.

All this diversity awaits you, but it is better not to be one of Zeus's buzzards. Somerset is no place for a quick fly-by, it is a county for walking.

Using this book

Right: Cheddar Gorge (Walk 40)

Pinkery Pond to Moles Chamber

Experience quintessential Exmoor among the barrows and tumuli of its Bronze Age farmers.

DISTANCE *5.75 miles (9.2km)*   MINIMUM TIME *3hrs*

ASCENT/GRADIENT *700ft (213m)* ▲▲▲   LEVEL OF DIFFICULTY +++

PATHS *Narrow moorland paths following fences and some tracks, I stile*

LANDSCAPE *Bleak, grassy moorland*

SUGGESTED MAP *OS Explorer OL 9 Exmoor*

START / FINISH *Grid reference: SS 729401*

DOG FRIENDLINESS *Be aware of possible livestock, ponies and deer on open moorland*

PARKING *Unmarked roadside pull-off on B3358 on Goat Hill*

PUBLIC TOILETS *None en route; nearest in Simonsbath car park*

Chains Barrow is the highest point on the waterlogged Exmoor plateau of purple moor grass and deer sedge. Other walks hereabouts are Exmoor more or less; this one is Exmoor pure and simple. It has views out to the sea and to the sheltered lands below. It's a walk for a sunny day with skylarks, or for a chill one in autumn. In cloud and rain, with the bog at full squelch, you absorb a lot of atmosphere (and quite a bit of the rain), though this may not be everyone's idea of fun.

Bronze Age Exmoor

In about 2000 BC the hunter-gatherer lifestyle of the Stone Age came to an end on Exmoor. In the Bronze Age that followed we find traces of agriculture, with crops, such as barley, and livestock (mostly cattle and sheep). We also find the round barrows, for example, Chains Barrow and Longstone Barrow, scattered across the moorland summits. Elsewhere in Somerset the standing stones are of the Bronze Age – charred wood accidentally buried under the stones can be carbon-dated. More doubtfully, Tarr Steps in the south of Exmoor are also credited to the Bronze-Age people (see Walk 3).

It used to be thought that the change from the Stone Age to the Bronze Age came about by conquest: better swords and axes allowed the new people to kill or enslave the old. Today, tree pollen preserved in peat bogs can be dated very accurately, and shows that the clearance of the moors for farming was a gradual process. The scratch-plough was perhaps more important than the sword: experts believe that it was the idea of sitting still and starting a farm that conquered, rather than a particular tribe. The climate was warmer and drier in those days, and the moorland was grass rather than peat. Large areas will have been hedged and banked for pasture: on Dartmoor, 25,000 acres (10,000ha) of Bronze Age-enclosures have been mapped out.

High Society

The shepherds belonged to a wider social unit than the family or farmstead. At least some of the people in charge had enough

THE CHAINS

importance to build up a substantial collections of 50 or 60 axe heads, implying that the Bronze Age farmers weren't entirely peaceful people. Someone else had enough spare time to build the long barrows and raise the standing stones, and there were jewellers working in jadeite and bronze.

It isn't known why Bronze Age people chose to build their barrows here on the bleakest of hilltops. Perhaps they were scared of the spirits of the dead and wanted to keep them out of the way, or perhaps a really large, conspicuous barrow would intimidate the people on the next hill.

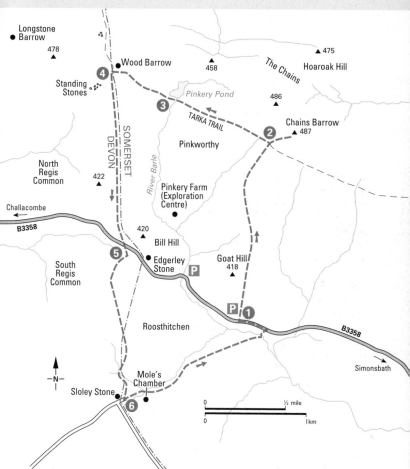

WALK 1 DIRECTIONS

❶ At the Simonsbath end of the pull-off is a gate with a bridleway sign for Chains Barrow. Go up the right-hand edges of two fields, then head 35yds (32m) left, to a gate. The way across the following rough moorland is marked by occasional blue-topped posts. Walk gently uphill, keeping parallel with a hedge away on the left. The marked way bends slightly right, up the crest of a wide moorland spur. At the top is a bank with a gateway.

THE CHAINS

② A signpost indicates a sketchy path out over the moor to Chains Barrow. Return to the gateway and follow the path ahead, signed 'Pinkery Pond', running along and above the fenced bank. It leads across the moor top to Pinkery Pond; this is crossed on its dam.

③ Follow the fence as it continues uphill to a gate with a blue spot. Maintain your direction across moorland for 350yds (320m) to join a high bank and fence from the right, and follow this to Wood Barrow.

WHAT TO LOOK OUT FOR

The Lynton & Barnstaple Railway, above Parracombe, currently runs just 1 mile (1.6km) across the very top of Exmoor, giving passengers wonderfully wide views westwards across Devon. There are ambitious plans to extend its narrow guage steam service to the original terminus at Barnstaple.

④ The gate ahead leads into Devon. Beyond, Wood Barrow is one of many put to more conventional use, originally by the Saxons, as markers of the Devon boundary. In front of Woodbarrow Gate turn left on a signed bridleway track, with a high bank on its right. This leads off the moor. Bear left around a sheep-pen made of disused metal crash barriers.

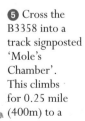 A gate leads on to the B3358.

⑤ Cross the B3358 into a track signposted 'Mole's Chamber'. This climbs for 0.25 mile (400m) to a

The Exmoor Steam Railway runs steam trains along a mile (1.6km) of narrow gauge track above Bratton Fleming. It's England's highest narrow gauge railway, with wide views over the valley of the Devon Yeo.

signpost. Here you must bear left, keeping to the left of a fence, for 550yds (503m). A junction of high banks soon comes into sight: take the gate ahead and go downhill to the left of the high bank beyond. Go straight downhill to the right-hand of two narrow gates, with a stream and the start of a track beyond. Follow this up and to the right, to just before the corner of a tarred road. An inscribed boundary marker, the Sloley Stone, is just above the track.

⑥ Turn down sharp left, away from the road. A faint old track runs down across a stream to a narrow gate with a blue paint-spot. An improving path runs down to the right of the stream, gradually slanting up to a gate. Here join a larger track, and immediately after the gate keep ahead, slanting slightly downhill. A faint green track runs parallel with the river down on the left, to a signposted gate. Turn left on a concrete track, to join the B3358. Turn left to the parking pull-off.

WHERE TO EAT AND DRINK

The Exmoor Forest Inn at Simonsbath serves good food and Exmoor Ale (brewed in Wiveliscombe, see Walk 16), but clean dogs are welcome. The bar is decorated with bits of dead animals. Indeed, this is your best chance of sighting a badger: there's a stuffed one climbing the wall above the fireplace.

Down the Doone Valley

Fact and fiction intertwine in this moorland valley walk which visits the tiny church celebrated in R D Blackmore's classic novel.

DISTANCE *8.75 miles (14.1km)*   **MINIMUM TIME** *4hrs 30min*

ASCENT/GRADIENT *1,250ft (380m)* ▲▲▲   **LEVEL OF DIFFICULTY** +++

PATHS *Some steep ground, pathless open moor*

LANDSCAPE *Bleak, grassy moor, then a charming enclosed valley*

SUGGESTED MAP *OS Explorer OL 9 Exmoor*

START / FINISH *Grid reference: SS 820464*

DOG FRIENDLINESS *Well-controlled – livestock throughout, horse riders in Doone Valley*

PARKING *Car park (free) at Robbers Bridge*

PUBLIC TOILETS *None en route; toilets at County Gate on A39*

It is not often that a fictional place gets mapped in black print by the Ordnance Survey. But the area of Exmoor where Somerset and Devon meet is marked on the Explorer map as 'Doone Country'; and paths leading towards Badgworthy Water are signposted 'Doone Valley'.

Near the foot of the valley is a monument to the man responsible, Richard Doddridge Blackmore (1825–1900), 'whose novel *Lorna Doone* extols to all the world the joys of Exmoor'. Badgworthy Water is not really Doone Valley. There's no point in trying to work out which window of Oare church is the one Carver pointed his carbine through to shoot Lorna on her wedding day – Carver never existed, so didn't need a window.

In some strange way Blackmore's Exmoor is more real and romantic than the flat Exmoor of fact. The angle at the top of the Badgworthy (grid reference SS 795434) really is Doone Gate, defended with a barrier and a tunnel – here Jan Ridd and Jeremy Stickles made their disastrous assault in Chapter 54. Walking down the valley, we mentally move the medieval village into the main valley, and place the small house of the sinister Counsellor Doone across the stream itself. At the same time we must raise the valley walls higher, and add rocks and crags to the slopes of heather, hawthorn and gorse that we see in the real world.

As for the enclosed and dangerous waterslide that Jan Ridd clambers up to meet his Lorna, that won't be found at all, unless it's in the side valley of Lank Combe. Exmoor has bogs, but none of them is the Wizard's Slough, deep enough to swallow up the mighty Carver Doone. And there are no gold mines. It's at Oare church that romance and reality come together, for the building is virtually as it is in Blackmore's book, and one John Ridd was churchwarden there no longer ago than 1925.

The Doones of Badgworthy

The Doones of Badgworthy existed in local legend before Lorna Doone, certainly as a story to scare naughty children, and possibly in fact. Lawless men did take refuge on Exmoor in the aftermath of the Civil War and the

DOONE VALLEY

Monmouth Rebellion. However, they could scarcely have plundered the countryside and murdered its inhabitants for a full century without ever appearing in the law court records of the time.

WALK 2 DIRECTIONS

❶ Cross Robber's Bridge and follow the road to Oareford. Turn left up the bridleway track signed 'Larkbarrow'. After a mile (1.6km), the now faint track runs straight up across two grassy fields to a signposted gate where

a bridleway from Oare church joins the route. Keep ahead up this third field over its rounded crest, and bear slightly left to a gate at its back left corner.

❷ Go through a gate on the left, and then a narrow gate on the right to rougher moorland.

DOONE VALLEY

Take a faint path ahead for 140yds (128m). Here bear slightly right on a smaller path to go through a shallow col or gap. Now a wider path arrives from the right. Bear left on it to large and small wooden gates.

3 The path ahead leads down, with a bank on its left, to Edwards Post. Turn right ('Badgworthy Valley') on a clear path that gradually climbs to a gate. It then drops towards the Badgworthy Valley, rises again, then drops to cross the railed footbridge at Doone Gate.

4 A wide path continues downstream. After a plank footbridge a gate leads into the hummocks of the lost medieval village. Go straight up to a wide path and turn right. Continue down the main valley, through woods, to a large footbridge to Cloud Farm.

5 Pass to the left of Cloud Farm, on to a track that passes through a farm shed, then climbs out of the valley. Where it ends, follow the lower side of a field to the edge of a wooded combe. Turn right for 70yds (64m) to a gate on the left. A track passes above the combe and turns down beyond it. Where the track bends right, keep

WALK 2

WHAT TO LOOK OUT FOR

The outlines of the former Badgworthy village are visible under the bracken above the foot of Hoccombe Combe. The buildings are the two-room long house, with cattle on one side and people on the other. The last inhabitant, a shepherd, is said to have died in a blizzard with his little granddaughter around 1800.

downhill through waymarked gates, to turn left on the valley road below beside Oare church.

6 Turn right, signposted 'Porlock', and follow the road for 130yds (118m) to cross Oare Water. Turn right along the riverside to ford a small stream. A few paces further on, turn up left to a small summer house and then turn right between gorse bushes. A grass path leads straight up a sharp spur. It continues beside a fence to a gate; keep ahead, across heather, to the right-hand corner of a plantation.

7 Turn right on a small track ('Oareford'). This bends left near a field corner; here keep ahead, past a blue-topped post on a path towards some tall trees. Pass to the right of these trees, which mark ancient field-edges, to a small gate. A path leads steeply down to a footbridge into Oareford. Turn left to return to your car.

WHILE YOU'RE THERE

Oare church needed no added romance from RD Blackmore, even if he did have to put in an extra window. In 800 years of extensions, decorations and repairs, nothing ugly has found its way into this tiny church. The eye travels happily from the Norman font to the buzzard lectern, carved as recently as 1999. Among many small treasures, I particularly like the cherubic memorials of 1772 and 1791.

WHERE TO EAT AND DRINK

There are convenient tea rooms at Cloud Farm, near the end of the route, and just above where the waterslide in Chapter 7 of Lorna Doone would be (if it existed).

A Round of Applause for Tarr Steps

Visit one of the 'oldest' bridges in the world, set in a quiet valley clothed in ancient woodland.

DISTANCE 5.25 miles (8.4km)	**MINIMUM TIME** 2hrs 30min
ASCENT/GRADIENT 700ft (213m) ▲▲▲	**LEVEL OF DIFFICULTY** +++

PATHS Riverside paths and field tracks, some open moor, no stiles

LANDSCAPE Wooded river valley and pasture slopes above

SUGGESTED MAP OS Explorer OL 9 Exmoor

START / FINISH Grid reference: SS 872323

DOG FRIENDLINESS Dogs can run off-lead along River Barle

PARKING Just over 0.25 mile (400m) east of Tarr Steps – can be full in summer. (Parking at Tarr Steps for disabled people only.)

PUBLIC TOILETS At car park

This is the longest and best clapper stone bridge in Britain; as such it featured on a postage stamp in 1968. (The others in the set were the stone military bridge at Aberfeldy; Telford's Menai Bridge; and a concrete viaduct on the M4.) Bronze Age trackways converge on to this river crossing, suggesting that the bridge itself may be about 4,000 years old. Given that it gets swept away and rebuilt after every major flood, this date for its construction is pure guesswork – or, to use the archaeological term, 'conjectural'. It is still arguably Europe's oldest bridge.

'Cleaca' Bridge
The name 'clapper' probably comes from the Saxon 'cleaca', meaning stepping stones. The first clapper bridges arose as stone slabs laid across the top of existing stepping stones. With a serviceable ford alongside, this one is clearly a luxury rather than a necessity. It is only because the local sedimentary rocks form such suitable slabs that it was built at all. At 59yds (54m), Tarr Steps is by far the longest of the 40 or so clapper bridges left in Britain.

Right of Way
As the bridge is a public highway you could, in theory, be entitled to ride your bicycle across it. (I have seen this done, though not tried it myself.) Quite clearly, the damage you might do to yourself by falling off the bridge could be very serious. That said, the feat is not as hard as it looks – the secret seems to lie in avoiding catching the front wheel in the slots where the bridge top consists of two separate, parallel stones. The ford alongside is popular with horse-riders and canoeists, though *The Highway Code* does not seem to specify who gives way when the one meets the other. It's always very pleasing to see these three non-motorised forms of transport in action together, while motorists are unable to make it down the congested narrow road.

The Woods

Local legend gives the bridge a devilish origin. Apparently Satan himself built it for sunbathing on. The shady groves of ancient woodland, that drove him into the middle of the river, form probably the best birding terrain in the country – you need only to sit or stand quietly in the shadow of a tree trunk and wait for the birds to parade before you. It's also good for the birds, offering them safety from hawks and buzzards, plenty of nest sites, insects to eat and open flight paths between the branches.

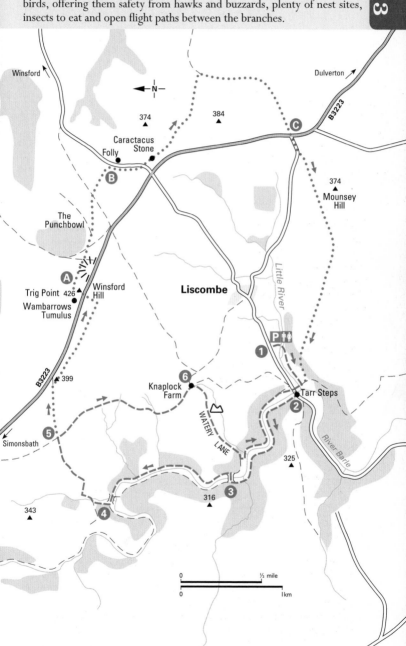

WALK 3 DIRECTIONS

❶ Leave the bottom of the car park by the left-hand junction, signposted 'Scenic Path'. This takes you down to the left of the road to the Little River, crossing two footbridges on its way to Tarr Steps, over the River Barle, ahead.

❷ Cross the Steps, turning upstream at the far side (signed 'North Barton Wood'). Follow a wide river bank path past what looks like a wire footbridge but is, in fact, a device for intercepting floating trees in times of flood. After 0.75 mile (1.2km) cross a side-stream on a stone bridge (mini Tarr Steps), and immediately afterwards a long footbridge over the River Barle.

❸ Cross, and continue upstream, with the river now on the left. After 0.75 mile (1.2km) the path crosses a small wooden footbridge, and then divides at a signpost.

❹ Turn right, uphill, signed 'Winsford Hill'. A wide path goes up through the woods with a stream on its right. Where it meets a track turn briefly right to ford the stream, then continue uphill on a narrower signed path. At a low bank with beech trees turn right to a gate and follow the foot of a field to a tarred lane. Go up this to a cattle grid on to open moor. Here, bear right on a faint track that heads up between gorse bushes. After 250yds (229m) it reaches a 4-way signpost.

❺ Turn right ('Knaplock') and slant down to a hedge corner. The route follows the foot of the open moor, but is about to divert up left to avoid some bog. After 170yds (155m) a sign points back down to the moor-foot banking. A beech bank crosses ahead: aim for a gate at the lower end of this, where a soft track leads forward, with occasional blue paint-spots. After 0.25 mile (400m) the track turns downhill, then back to the left. It becomes firmer and drier as it reaches Knaplock Farm.

❻ Among the farm buildings turn downhill signed 'Tarr Steps', to exit on a muddy farm track. This develops into a steep, narrow and stony track, Watery Lane. After its initial descent it becomes a smooth path down to the River Barle. Turn left, downstream. When the path rises a little above the river, look out for a fork on the right, signed 'Footpath'. This rejoins the river to pass through an open field that's just right for a more comfortable sunbathe than the busy Tarr Steps. Cross the road and a small footbridge, then turn left up the path to your car.

Winsford Hill

*High above Tarr Steps, join the ponies
on the heathy hill.*

See map and information panel for Walk 3

DISTANCE *7.75 miles (12.5km)*   **MINIMUM TIME** *3hrs 45min*

ASCENT/GRADIENT *1,000ft (305m)* ▲▲▲   **LEVEL OF DIFFICULTY** ✚✚✚

WALK 4 DIRECTIONS
(Walk 3 option)

At Point ❺ keep ahead, signed B3223. The green track slants up through gorse, thorn bushes and some heather. With the railing of the B3223 road visible just above, fork right on to a track that runs gently uphill. This keeps parallel with the road and well below it. You may spot a quartz outcrop just below the track. At its highest point the track narrows between gorse bushes and, 100yds (91m) further on, a small path turns up to the left. This leads to the road: cross it to the trig point on Winsford Hill, Point ❹.

Continue ahead, towards Dunkery Hill (which fills the northern horizon), for just 35yds (33m), then right, on a green track that runs gently downhill to the head of the deep Punchbowl hollow on the left. Here the main path bears slightly left and continues level – ignore smaller paths descending further to the left. Keep ahead over the crest of a gentle ridge, and down to the lane (Point ❸) opposite 'Folly House'.

The path continues immediately above the road, on its right. At a 'Give way' sign, cross the road to the shelter around the Caractacus Stone. The path continues just to the right of a high hedge bank

crossing the moor. Where a track arrives from below, follow it uphill briefly, then fork off left, again keeping the hedge bank on your left. After another 0.5 mile (800m) you pass under scattered trees; then as the hedge bends left continue ahead to reach a signpost at a road junction, Point ❻.

Cross to a minor road, shortly leading to a cattle grid. Here keep ahead on a track between gateposts. After 100yds (91m) bear left at a sign for Tarr Steps, on to a rougher track. After a gate with a signpost the path bears slightly right, away from a hedge on the left. Opposite the start-point car park, just continue the gentle descent into birch woods. At the foot of the slope the path reaches a small gate and a leafy, sunken way down to the River Barle. Turn right for a few steps to Tarr Steps, and turn up to the right (before the footbridge) on the scenic path.

Right: Winsford Hill (Walk 4)

Withypool's River and Common

A short walk up the wooded riverside and on to the grassy moorland.

DISTANCE *3.5 miles (5.7km)* MINIMUM TIME *1hr 45min*

ASCENT/GRADIENT *350ft (107m)* ▲▲▲ LEVEL OF DIFFICULTY +++

PATHS *Narrow riverside path, field paths and open moor, 17 stiles*

LANDSCAPE *Small moorland valley*

SUGGESTED MAP *OS Explorer OL 9 Exmoor*

START / FINISH *Grid reference: SS 844354*

DOG FRIENDLINESS *Appropriate control over fields, riverside and moorland*

PARKING *Small car park (free, busy on summer weekends) just across river from Withypool village*

PUBLIC TOILETS *In village centre, opposite shop*

WALK 5 DIRECTIONS

The upper Barle Valley is the heart of Exmoor: not dramatic combes and sudden seaside, but a gentle and rather melancholy landscape.

A small gate leads out of the car park to the River Barle. Turn left, following the river bank upstream. Withypool, with its wooded brook, lies below long grass slopes and the bare moorland plateau. The walk will make its way up the River Barle for about 1.5 miles (2.4km), gradually working up through fields away from the stream. At the edge of moorland it will turn back to return along the top of the enclosed lands.

The bare moorland plateau is characterised by a quiet that may be disturbed by the occasional whinny of a pony. Ponies have been on Exmoor for longer than people: they are the closest there is to the original wild horse of Europe. A hundred years ago they came close to extinction. We have Sir Thomas Dyke Ackland, the

landowner who leased Winsford Hill to the National Trust, to thank for their continued existence.

Today there are only about 1,000 of these ponies in the world. The 150 ponies on Exmoor are in 11 herds, two of them in the care of the National Park Authority.

The waymarked path crosses a stile and a footbridge, then passes through a gate into a short, hedged way. After a stile it follows the left edge of two fields, below the big shed of Waterhouse Farm, to a stile. Now bear slightly left to a stile with a hedged track going uphill beyond. This track will be our return route. At the track

WHILE YOU'RE THERE

A couple of miles (3.2km) upstream is Landacre Bridge – you could include it in your walk, or drive there afterwards. Its medieval stonework has proved strong enough for today's traffic. There are picnic spots alongside the River Barle.

foot turn right to a stile. Cross a field next to a railed fence on the right, with a narrow strip of wild meadowsweet along the river bank beyond. At the corner cross a stone footbridge to a wooden one, and continue on the river bank. Ignore two kissing gates on the left, but cross a stile ahead into an open field.

At the end of this field turn uphill at a signpost on a faint path with a hedge on the right, to a corner gap. Here another sign points towards Brightworthy Farm. Pass through gates immediately to the right of the buildings, into a fenced-off path around a field-edge. A bridge on the left leads to steps down into a earth track. Turn right and, as the track fades out, pass a concrete shed to follow the bottom edges of two fields. The moorland is one field above, and the river now about two fields below. Through a field gate in the corner, the trench of a trackway descends gently to a gate leading to the open moor.

You are most likely to see ponies at quiet times of the day. They live wild on the moors year-round. Evolution has given them a thick weatherproof coat, tough hooves, and a raised ridge around the eye (the so-called 'toad eye') to cast off rain, as well as enough speed and endurance to escape from the sabre-tooth tiger that once hunted them. But every Exmoor pony belongs to someone and every autumn they are gathered, inspected for disease and branded.

From here you could extend your walk to the medieval Landacre Bridge, soon visible 0.5 mile (800m) ahead – a suitable spot for your picnic. Otherwise turn left, following a sign for Withypool Common. A faint, rutted path follows the hedge that forms the boundary of the enclosed ground. After an initial climb, it bends left and levels off.

The path gets clearer, and follows the hedge bank just below. It crosses a tarred driveway running down into the fields. Soon afterwards you encounter the steep-sided stream valley of Knighton Combe. The path slants down to the right and crosses the stream at a shallow ford.

Head downstream for about 100yds (91m) between rowans, then slant up the combe side to rejoin the field-top hedge. The path is now clear, running towards the road that runs down into Withypool. About 220yds (201m) before the road turn down left to a stile with paint spot in a corner of the hedge. A lane runs downhill to a gate. Cross this and the stile ahead to rejoin the outward route. Turn right and continue downstream to Withypool Bridge.

Wimbleball Lake and Haddon Hill

Natural and artificial landscapes merge on this route through wooded valley, heathy hill and across the mighty Wimbleball Dam.

WALK 6

DISTANCE *6 miles (9.7km)*   MINIMUM TIME *3hrs*

ASCENT/GRADIENT *750ft (230m)* ▲▲▲   LEVEL OF DIFFICULTY +++

PATHS *Rough descent, long climb, easy track between, 2 stiles*

LANDSCAPE *Deeply wooded valley followed by airy, open heathland*

SUGGESTED MAP *OS Explorer OL 9 Exmoor*

START / FINISH *Grid reference: SS 969285*

DOG FRIENDLINESS *On lead for short section past Haddon Hill Farm, no swimming (dogs or people)*

PARKING *Frogwell Lodge car park, Haddon Hill*

PUBLIC TOILETS *At car park*

You'll probably find it hard to imagine an outward force of 3.3 tons per square foot (36 tonnes per square metre) but that is the force exerted by the waters of Wimbleball Lake against the wall which contains them.

Wimbleball Dam

Some 200,000 tons of crushed stone from a quarry at Bampton was used to construct the dam in the mid-1970s. Sand from Cullompton was chosen to impart a pinkish colour and match the local bedrock. It's made of concrete, though the surface texture vaguely imitates massive stonework; and the 13 buttresses have no particular structural purpose but, aesthetically, they prevent it from looking too huge. The dam took four years to build, and the reservoir behind it needed another year just to fill up.

Water Cycled and Recycled

The reservoir holds almost 5 billion gallons (23 billion litres), which is enough to supply the whole South West peninsula for 44 days, or a town like Bridgwater for nine and a half years. Its main job is to store water from the winter through into summer. It is also used to maintain the water level in the River Exe. When the river is full, a pipeline pumps water from Exebridge near Dulverton up into the reservoir. For the rest of the time the same pipeline, working the other way, delivers water to Dulverton. And, when it's really dry, the reservoir releases water into the Haddeo below the dam and so back into the Exe. Some of this will be water that had already flowed down the Exe during the previous winter.

A Multi-purpose Reservoir

Some 50 years ago water boards took the view that humans were dirty beasts who shouldn't be allowed anywhere near their own drinking water. However, Wimbleball was planned from the start to provide not only drinking water but also recreation: fishing water, sailing water and walk-around-it water. (If you've half a day to spare, you can do a complete circuit

WIMBLEBALL LAKE

on a waymarked path.) The woodland that looks so natural was planned by landscape architect Dame Sylvia Crowe and planted just 30 years ago, with the trees around the car park being the first to go in. Sadly, nothing can be done about the ugly and barren foreshore, since no plant can establish itself on ground that is submerged for months at a time. But, thanks to careful management, the weird, rattling cry of the nightjar now floats across the crystal clear and still drinking water.

To finish with, here are some more numbers to ponder as you are walking: 1.5 million people live downstream from Wimbleball Lake and drink its water, but every year 2 million sail on it, fish from it, or just walk down to its shores to have a look.

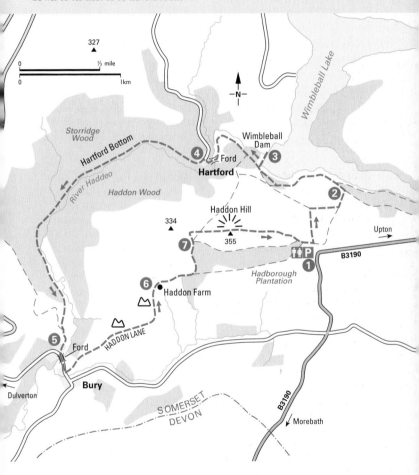

WALK 6 DIRECTIONS

❶ Leave the car park by a kissing gate, which overlooks the reservoir. The earth path down ahead crosses another earth track, and runs down towards the reservoir to meet a tarred track.

(Left down this track leads to the dam, Point ❸.) Cross and turn right, on a rough track contouring to the right. After 350yds (320m) this enters scattered birches. Turn down left, on a smaller path, to meet a stony track just above the reservoir.

2 Turn left on this. It emerges into open grassland and starts rising to the left. Watch out for a stile down on the right, into woodland. Across this, turn left on a small path that emerges near the Wimbleball Dam. A side-trip on to the dam gives fine views of Hartford Bottom below.

WHERE TO EAT AND DRINK

Lowtrow Cross Inn is on the B3190, 2 miles (3.2km) east of Wheddon Hill car park. It's an old drover's halt, and in a sense carries on the trade, though travellers now park caravans, not cows, in the field alongside. There is a conveniently placed summer tea shop at Cowlings on the west side of the reservoir.

3 Return along the dam and turn right into a descending tarmac lane signed 'Bury 2.5'. At the bottom keep ahead on a concrete path signed 'Bridleway'. With a bridge ahead, bear left on to a grass track, this time signposted 'Bridleway to Bury'. It leads to a ford, so watch out for the footbridge on the right. Once across, take a track between houses, to turn left out into Hartford.

4 Turn left ('Bury 2') on a well-used track. It passes through woods of oak and beech beside the River Haddeo. The track becomes tarmac as it enters the charming little village of Bury.

WHILE YOU'RE THERE

Dulverton, the capital of Exmoor, remains an attractive small town. It has a very good selection of cafés and pubs, and the Exmoor National Park Centre in Fore Street is a useful entry point for the National Park.

5 Turn left to the packhorse bridge beside the road's ford. Ignore a riverside track on the left and continue for 180yds (165m) to turn left at a bridleway sign, 'Haddon Hill'. Here pass between houses and ahead into a sunken track. This climbs steeply, with a stream at the bottom that flows over orange bedrock. At the top it continues as a green (or brown) track between grown-out hedges, before turning left for another short climb to reach Haddon Farm.

6 Pass to the left of the farmhouse, on its access track. After 0.25 mile (400m) this reaches the corner of a wood. As the track is concreted on a steep section, look out for a stile above leading into the wood. Go up the left-hand side of the wood to reach a gate on to the open hill at its top corner.

7 Take a track that bears left to cross the crest of the hill. With views ahead to Brompton Regis, turn sharp right, on a wide track that runs to the top of Haddon Hill. Continue downhill, on a wide track through open moor of gorse and heather, to the car park.

WHAT TO LOOK OUT FOR

Haddon Hill is the largest area of heathland in the Brendons. In June or July you may see the heath fritillary. This is a fairly small butterfly, coloured brown and reddish-orange; within the UK it flies only in a few scattered spots in the far south.

Hawk Combe and Porlock Hill

A stiff climb through the wildwood for a sudden sea view.

WALK 7

DISTANCE *6 miles (9.7km)* MINIMUM TIME *3hrs 15min*

ASCENT/GRADIENT *1,200ft (366m)* ▲▲▲ LEVEL OF DIFFICULTY +++

PATHS *Initial stiff climb then smooth, well-marked paths, no stiles*

LANDSCAPE *Steep woodland, leading on to open heath*

SUGGESTED MAP *OS Explorer OL 9 Exmoor*

START / FINISH *Grid reference: SS 885468*

DOG FRIENDLINESS *Deer and wild ponies so dogs must be under control*

PARKING *Pay-and-display at Porlock Central Car Park; free parking at Whitstone Post, Point* ⑤

PUBLIC TOILETS *At car park*

A wood used to be something that just happened: a patch of ground too steep for the plough and too far from the village to be cut for firewood. Sometimes a patch of trees in a field corner turns out to have been there since the ancient wildwood covered the land at the end of the ice age. This is shown by the number and variety of its plant species, in particular its lichens; and by certain sorts of tree, such as the small-leaved lime. The Exmoor coast is rich in such woodland and in Hawk Combe the woods are among the oldest in Somerset.

Ancient Oaks

On the sandstone soils and under the warm rainfall of the Exmoor combes the natural cover is an oak wood, specifically sessile oak. The more familiar common oak has its acorns on stalks, while the sessile's ones grow straight on the twig; in addition, the sessile oak's leaves are longer and less rounded than those of the common oak.

Under the oaks grow native shrubs such as hazel and whitebeam. Our many sorts of native woodlice, leaf aphids and tree creepers flourish best on our native trees: they don't like nasty 'foreign' food like the horse chestnut. Dormice live in the hazel thickets, and the pied flycatcher darts through the green gloom. This bird prefers the western woods – some naturalists say that this is because the sessile oak, being lower and more spreading, gives better flight paths; others think it's just because these woods are allowed more creative neglect: rotten branches drop off, leaving handy nest holes.

Porlock Hill

If the climb through the woods of Hawk Combe is steep for feet, the A39 is equally so for wheels. It climbs 800ft in a mile (24m in 1.6km), with the steepest bit at the bottom. Extra horses were stationed at Porlock for attaching to the coaches here. Two-thirds of the way up until recently stood a traditional AA phone box in black, retained as a memory of the days when steam would jet from your radiator and the helpful AA man would

PORLOCK

come on his motorbike with a can of water. Modern cars can manage the ascent, though drivers who stall their engines may still have considerable trouble with a hill start on a 1 in 4 (25%) gradient. Coming down, though, there's still potential energy to be got rid of at roughly the rate of a one-bar electric fire. Those who neglect to engage low gear will end up with very hot brake discs – in Porlock car park you may catch the burnt-toast aroma of a car recently arrived from the west.

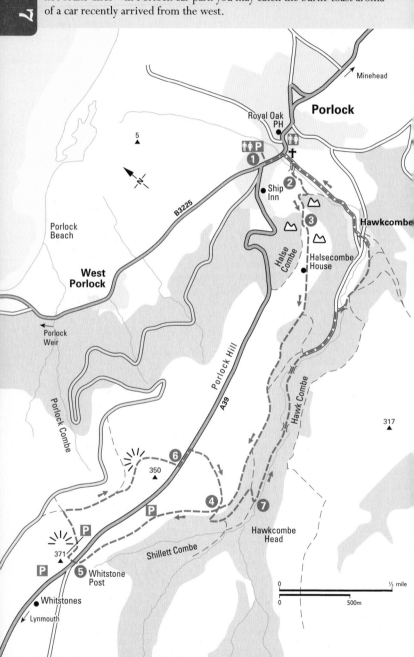

WALK 7 DIRECTIONS

1 Leave the car park at its top end, then turn left. Just before the church turn right into Parsons Street. At a small parking area a bridleway sign for Hawkcombe points upstream to a footbridge.

2 The path climbs through bamboo and laurel, to join another bridleway. This zig-zags steeply up through the wood, to pass below a wall with a small inset bench. At the top of this low wall, the paths then divide.

3 Turn left, still climbing, and at once bear left, signposted 'Hawkcombe', into a sunken path. Emerging at a white house, called

Halsecombe, keep ahead to a field gate marked with a blue spot. Follow the left edge of a field, to the right-hand of two gates; the next gate ahead leads back into woodland. Take the bridleway track ahead, gently descending. It becomes a terraced path, running near the top edge of the wood for a mile (1.6km) to reach a track.

4 Turn left down the track for just a few paces, and then turn right up a path between gorse bushes; it then runs through bracken and heather with views into the head of Hawk Combe. As the path enters a thicket of hawthorns bear right to reach the road signpost at Whitstone Post.

5 Cross the A39 into a parking area, and turn right down a heather path parallel with the road. After 110yds (100m) turn left down a broad track. Where it turns left, turn right on to a smaller track. This contours through gorse and heather, then rejoins the A39 at a cattle grid.

6 Turn left, then right on a track signposted to Hawkcombe. Cross two cattle grids to reach Point **4** of the outward route. Keep on the track for another 125yds (114m), then turn left into a small, terraced path. This runs gently downhill for 0.25 mile (400m), to meet a wider path. Turn sharp right down to the stream.

7 A broad path runs downstream. On reaching some houses it becomes a tarred lane and descends through a wood. At a high wall on the right a footpath sign points to a footbridge. Over this, the path ascends gently through the woods for 220yds (201m). Bear left on a crossing path and gently descend to a street. Turn left to cross the stream, then turn right into Parsons Street and Porlock.

Overleaf: Porlock and Hawk Combe (Walk 7)

Horner's Corners

On the trail of Exmoor's red deer in the woodlands under Dunkery Beacon.

DISTANCE 4.5 miles (7.2km)	**MINIMUM TIME** 2hrs 30min
ASCENT/GRADIENT 1,000ft (305m) ▲▲▲	**LEVEL OF DIFFICULTY** +++
PATHS Broad paths, with some stonier ones, steep in places, no stiles	
LANDSCAPE Dense woodland in steep-sided stream valleys	
SUGGESTED MAP OS Explorer OL 9 Exmoor	
START / FINISH Grid reference: SS 898455	
DOG FRIENDLINESS Off lead, but be aware of deer and horse-riders	
PARKING National Trust car park (free) at Horner	
PUBLIC TOILETS At car park	

Horner takes its name from the Saxon 'hwrnwr', a wonderfully expressive word meaning snorer, that here describes the rumble of the stream in its enclosed valley. Above the treetops, Webber's Post is a splendid viewpoint out across the Bristol Channel. What Mr Webber stood there to view, though, was the hunting of red deer.

The herd on Exmoor numbers several thousand. Although this is small compared to those in the Scottish Highlands, the Exmoor stag himself is the UK's biggest wild deer. This is simply because his life is slightly easier – farmed deer are larger again. On Exmoor, as in the rest of Northern Europe outside Scotland, the deer remains a forest animal. Exmoor's mix of impenetrable woodland with areas of open grazing, even with all its houses, farms and fields, remains good deer country.

The calf is born dappled for camouflage under the trees, and lies in shelter during the day while the hind feeds. If you do come across a deer calf, leave it alone – it hasn't been abandoned. During the summer the stags and hinds run in separate herds. In the Scottish Highlands deer graze on high ground during the day to escape from midges, and descend to the forest at night; on Exmoor the main annoying pest is the human, so the deer graze the moor at dawn and dusk, and spend the day in the trees.

Stag Nights

In September and October comes the spectacular rut, when stags roar defiance at each other, and, if that fails, do battle with antlers for mating privileges. During this time they eat only occasionally, fight a lot and mate as often as possible. The stag with a mighty roar and a hard head can gather a harem of a dozen hinds. Your best chance of seeing one is very early or very late in the day – or else in the forest. You may well smell the deer, even though it probably smelled you first and has already gone quietly away. Look closely, too, at the small brown cows two fields away – they may well actually turn out to be deer – binoculars are a must.

While deer are thriving, it is the Exmoor stag hunters that are in danger of extinction. Just one pack of the traditional staghounds remains.

HORNER

Following pressure from its own members, the National Trust banned hunting from its land, and the national government has now criminalised it along with fox-hunting.

WALK 8 DIRECTIONS

❶ Leave the National Trust car park in Horner village past the toilets and turn right to the track leading into Horner Wood. This crosses a bridge and passes a field before rejoining Horner Water. You can take a footpath alongside the stream instead of the track,

they lead to the same place. Ignore the first footbridge, and continue along the obvious track to where a sign, 'Dunkery Beacon', points to the left towards a second footbridge.

❷ Ignore this footbridge as well (unless you're on Walk 9). Keep on the track for another 100yds

33

(91m), then fork left on a path alongside West Water. This rejoins the track, and after another 0.5mile (800m) alongside the track is another footbridge.

❸ Cross to a path that slants up to the right. After 200yds (183m) turn left into a smaller path that turns uphill alongside Prickslade Combe. The path reaches the combe's little stream at a cross-path, with the wood top visible above. Here turn left, across the stream, on a path contouring through the top of the wood. After a dip and climb, it emerges into the open and arrives at a fine view over the top of the woodlands to Porlock Bay. It joins a bridleway near a lone pine with a bench.

❹ Continue ahead on the bridleway's grassy track, with the car park of Webber's Post visible ahead. Alas, the deep valley of the East Water lies between you and your destination. So, in 55yds (50m), fork down left on a clear path back into birchwoods. This zig-zags down to meet a larger track in the valley bottom.

❺ Turn downstream, crossing a footbridge over the East Water, beside a ford. After about 60yds (55m) bear right on to an ascending path. At the top of the steep section turn right on a small sunken path that climbs to the right to Webber's Post car park.

❻ Walk to the left, round the car park, to a path to Horner. (Or you could take the pink-surfaced, easy-access path immediately to the right.) The path runs immediately below the 'easy access' one with its stone bench. Just after the concrete sculpture where easy access turns back, bear left on a wider path, soon passing a wooden shelter hut. Again fork left on a wider path to keep ahead down a wide, gentle spur, with the deep valley of the Horner Water on your left. As the spur steepens, the footpath meets a crossing track signposted 'Windsor Path'.

❼ Turn right for perhaps 30 paces, then take a descending path signposted 'Horner'. Narrow at first, this widens and finally meets a wide, horse-mangled track with wooden steps; turn left down this into Horner.

Fire at Dunkery Beacon

A moorland extension leads up to the high point of Somerset.

See map and information panel for Walk 8

DISTANCE 6 miles (9.7km) **MINIMUM TIME** 3hrs 40min

ASCENT/GRADIENT 1,706ft (520m) ▲▲▲ **LEVEL OF DIFFICULTY** +++

PATHS Rough paths in Horner Woods, stony hill descent, 1 stile

---

WALK 9 DIRECTIONS
(Walk 8 option)

At Point **2** of Walk 8, Point **A**, turn left over the bridge, signposted 'Dunkery Beacon'. A wide path leads up East Water, crossing to its left side by ford and footbridge. After 0.25 mile (400m) it crosses back, and in 45yds (40m) a path branches off on the right. It climbs in zig-zags, and then more gently, to a cross-track. Turn right to a pine tree and bench, Point **B**, (also Point **4** on Walk 8). Keep ahead, up to a gate. Follow the left edge of a field to another gate and stile, to a track to Cloutsham Farm. Turn left past the buildings, and, where the road bends, descend a track to rejoin the road lower down, Point **C**.

Turn up the road, past a picnic field. Just after a bridge on the left a stream runs down out of Aller Coombe and, 100yds (91m) further on, a wide path sets off across the stream, up the wooded spur. Fork right, through the first of three gates and on to the open hill, Point **D**.

Head uphill, to the right of Aller Coombe, on as clear path. After 120yds (110m) a contouring path crosses your own: this is Dicky's Path. To bypass Dunkery Hill simply turn left here to

pass through the woods of Aller Combe and continue from Point **F**; otherwise follow the clear path uphill. As the slope eases another path joins from the left – this will be your descent route. A moment later you top the rise and see just in front of you the huge cairn. Point **E**.

Nearby is a viewpoint cairn, with a topograph. Follow the ascent route back for 110yds (100m) and bear right on the path already noted. This runs down to the tip of Aller Coombe, now a mere groove in the heather. After another 25yds (23m) turn down left on a smaller path. After 600yds (549m) it passes three hawthorns and shortly a fourth one marks the junction with Dicky's Path, Point **F**.

Turn right on Dicky's Path, contouring through heather and thorn. It runs in and out of the steeply wooded Hollow Combe. Walk softly, for here you might see red deer. Emerge to open ground for 0.25 mile (400m). When Webbers Post car park appears ahead, fork left to reach it (Point **6**).

Overleaf: Dunkery Beacon (Walk 9)

Above the Severn Sea

*From Porlock to Minehead along paths
well-trodden by smugglers, coastguards
and a famous poet.*

DISTANCE *8 miles (12.9km)* MINIMUM TIME *4hrs*

ASCENT/GRADIENT *1,050ft (320m)* ▲▲▲ LEVEL OF DIFFICULTY +++

PATHS *Coast path, one steep, exposed, avoidable section, no stiles*

LANDSCAPE *Moorland, grassland and wood, high above sea*

SUGGESTED MAP *OS Outdoor Leisure 9 Exmoor*

START *Grid reference: SS 886467* FINISH *Grid reference: SS 972471*

DOG FRIENDLINESS *Open land, dogs must be under control*

PARKING *Pay-and-display all along Minehead seafront*

PUBLIC TOILETS *Porlock, Bossington, Minehead Harbour*

NOTE *Buses 37 and 300 run year-round, frequent service in summer;
from Minehead Station (beside the end of the railway lines)*

WALK 10 DIRECTIONS

From Porlock church take the main road back towards Minehead and turn left into Sparkhayes Lane. At the village end, steps on the right lead into Bay Road. At its end, turn left into a hedged path. Ignore kissing gates on the left to field paths. The well-used main path eventually leads to a lane, where you turn right into the thatched village of Bossington.

Pass to the right of the car park to a footbridge. A track on the left starts by the river, later climbs on to open hill. As it passes a National Trust collecting cairn note the path on the right climbing into Hurlstone Combe, before continuing ahead to the old coastguard viewpoint on Hurlstone Point.

During the 18th century, as a measure against smuggling, coastguards walked the coastal path, all night and in all weathers, one man for every quarter-mile

(400m). Almost every officer and man in the Royal Navy must have taken part either in smuggling or in its prevention. The resulting skill in foul weather seamanship and coastal raiding certainly contributed to the Navy's success against Napoleon Bonaparte.

The path ahead traverses a steep, exciting and atmospheric corner of the coastline. It should be avoided when slippery (after heavy rain) and in high winds: you may prefer to avoid it altogether. The alternative is to retrace your steps along the arrival path then fork left to a slightly higher one. Above the NT cairn, turn on to the path up Hurlstone Combe.

WHERE TO EAT AND DRINK

Beautifully placed at the corner of Minehead Harbour, the Old Ship Aground is pet-friendly and decorated with bits of real ships. The nearby Quayside Tearooms also welcome dogs.

WHAT TO LOOK OUT FOR

South West Coast Path walkers: those with the sea on their left will be on the last steps of their long walk. They'll be recognisable by their large rucksacks and weatherworn appearance. Those coming the other way will have a more eager air. Fewer than half of them will reach Poole Harbour.

Adventurous souls will continue from the lookout past a warning sign. The narrow path contours around the headland into a shallow combe formed by landslips. The path turns sharply back to the right, to zig-zag up the combe side. The spur above is rocky, so the path continues just down to the right of the crest, to the signpost at the head of Hurlstone Combe. Turn uphill on a broad path, eventually with the cairn of Selworthy Beacon ahead. In the dip before this, note where the coast path forks off to the left, but keep ahead to the top of Selworthy Beacon.

Return down the path for 80yds (73m) then fork right to rejoin the coast path. Follow its clear track just above enclosed pastures. Far out to sea you'll see the buildings of Bridgend in Wales. In the north-east are the islands of Flat Holm and Steep Holm. Flat Holm is in Wales, Steep Holm in England: their names reflect their profiles.

The Exmoor coast path was a favourite of Coleridge while living at Nether Stowey (see Walk 13). Three times he completed the 45 miles (72km) from the Quantocks to Lynton in a single day.

The track follows the foot of open moorland. It crosses the end of a tarred lane. After 0.5 mile (800m), above the V-notch of Grexy Combe, fork left on a softer track to stay along the moor foot. The way rises to a gate with a sign marking the end of the Holnicote Estate. This rises to a gate. Follow a coast path sign to keep on the same level for another 0.5 mile (800m), to a bench and signpost with a car park just above. Here take the steeper downhill fork, signed 'Coast Path Minehead Harbour'. After 200yds (183m) the path turns to the right, and becomes a splendid, broad and gentle terrace path, through a steep oakwood.

The South West Coast Path, at 600-odd miles (965km), is Britain's longest National Trail. This was achieved by re-establishing the coastguard path as a continuous right of way, a process which took the best part of 30 years. The result is a surprisingly steep and windy walk.

At a path junction and gate, turn down sharp left 'Coast Path Minehead', to the foot of the wood. Double back on a tarred

WHILE YOU'RE THERE

Exmoor Falconry and Animal Farm is just off the walk at Bossington. It has rabbits, ferrets and the chance to have an owl alight on your outstretched fist. It also offers full-day falconry outings on Exmoor.

track above the shoreline, fork left on to an earth track, and fork down left on a small path under holm oaks – all signed as Coast Path. A tarred shoreline path leads to Minehead Harbour. Ahead, along the shore road a pair of aluminium map-reading arms are the marker for the end or beginning of the rather longer coast path right round to Dorset.

From Wheddon Cross to Brendon's Heights

A sunken lane from Wheddon Cross leads up to Lype Hill, the high point of the Brendons.

DISTANCE 5.75 miles (9.2km)   MINIMUM TIME 3hrs

ASCENT/GRADIENT 850ft (260m) ▲▲▲   LEVEL OF DIFFICULTY +++

PATHS A rugged track, then little-used field bridleways, 2 stiles

LANDSCAPE Rounded hills with steep, wooded sides

SUGGESTED MAP OS Explorer OL 9 Exmoor

START / FINISH Grid reference: SS 923387

DOG FRIENDLINESS Mostly pasture, where dogs must be closely managed

PARKING Village car park (free) on A396 at Wheddon Cross

PUBLIC TOILETS At car park

This walk takes in the highest point of the Brendons, Lype Hill, at 1,388ft (423m). The wrap-around view includes Dunkery Beacon, Wales and Dartmoor. The trig point itself stands on an ancient tumulus; the second apparent tumulus nearby houses a modern-day water tank.

Brown Hill

Brendon means 'brown hill'. The shales and muddy sandstones are sea-bottom rocks: though the oldest in Somerset, they formed from the decomposition of still older mountains that have now disappeared. The Brendons are not particularly high, and are farmed to their tops, though the steeper sides are wooded. The scene appears timeless, but the hilltops were forested into the Middle Ages, and later became an industrial estate.

Return of the Iron Age

The Iron Age on Brendon saw the digging of long ramparts across the plateau, and a great settlement on the high ground. However, apart from a small fort at Elworthy Barrows, this activity wasn't in pre-Roman times, but in the more recent 19th century. A railway ran along the Brendon ridge from the iron ore mines. At its eastern end was a form of engineering we no longer see, except in Switzerland: a rope-assisted incline taking ore down to valley level. The ore then passed along the mineral railway to Watchet and the smelters of South Wales.

Below the mining areas and the farmland the hillsides have been less disturbed by man. Here, altitude, thin soils, and western levels of rainfall mean a sort of woodland more akin to the Scottish Highlands. You'll see the silver birch, for example – silver and gold if you're lucky enough to be here in late October. As well as a variety of autumn fungi in vivid colours, Hartcleeve has striking examples of Witch's Broom in its birch trees. These twig-clusters resemble untidy spherical nests but are in fact caused by a fungus infection (ascomycete) which interferes with the tree's growth hormones. A really well-established Witch's Broom can be 3ft (1m) across and will consist of hundreds of twigs.

The Sinking of Lanes

Putham Lane shows several centuries' worth of erosion in action: a speeded-up version of what's happening to the hills as a whole over millions of years (rather than a few hundred). Looking through the hedge you can see how much lower the lane is than the surrounding fields. Where the lane steepens, it also gets more deeply dug in; at its steepest point you can see bare grey bedrock in its floor. Where the track has dug itself down below the water table, a permanent stream trickles down it. After rain or during snowmelt this stream becomes a flood. Even at its low summer level, it's easy to see how it combines with feet (and, latterly, wheels) to excavate the track.

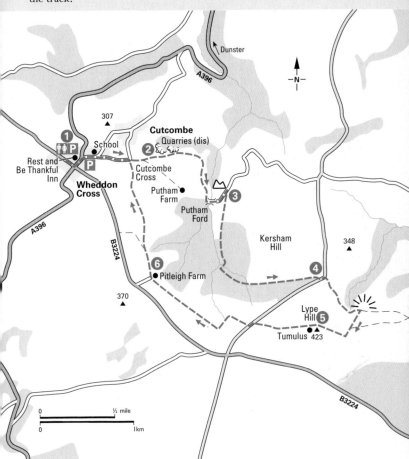

WALK 11 DIRECTIONS

❶ From the main crossroads head towards the village of Dunster, and bear right at the war memorial to pass a small car park on the right-hand side. After the school, bear right, following the signpost to Puriton. This is called Popery Lane – but no, the school we just passed was a Church of England one. The sunken lane runs to Cutcombe Cross, where you keep ahead ('Luxburough via Putham Ford') then bear left at a sign into Putham Lane.

WALK 11

2 Horses and tractors also use this narrow hedged track. At the bottom it crosses a ford, with a stone footbridge alongside. Now keep ahead on to a climbing lane surfaced with eroded tarmac.

3 At the top of the steep climb a field gate on the right has an footpath signpost, 'Lype Hill'. It leads on to a green track that runs below and then into a wood. A gate on the right leads to a less-used track. In 100yds (91m) turn down right across a stream, with yellow spots and posts marking the small path uphill to its right, into an open space. A slightly wider path above slants up along a bracken clearing. After a gate it follows the foot of a wood, to join a forest road and then reach a tarred lane.

4 Turn left, down a wide verge, and take the upper of two gates on the right: the correct one has a stile and footpath sign. Head up with beech bank on your left to cross the top of a wooded combe. Now a sea view is on the left, a stile and gate ahead. Don't cross, but turn right, and right again across the top of the field to a gate beside the trig point on Lype Hill.

5 Through the gate keep ahead across a field, with a tumulus 70yds (64m) away on the left, and after a gate bear left to follow the fence on the left to its corner. A gate ahead leads on to a road. Cross to a signposted gate, and

bear left to the field's far corner. Turn left alongside a beech bank to a waymarked gate. Don't go through the gate, but turn right along the fence to a smaller gate. Continue downhill with fences on your right and then a hedge on your left, towards the white-walled Pit Leigh Farm. A gate leads to the driveway just to the left of the farm.

6 Cross the driveway into a green track. This becomes a fenced-in field-edge to a gate on the left. Turn right to continue as before with hedges now on your right. After two fields you reach a hedged track. This runs down to the crossroads in Popery Lane and your return route to Wheddon Cross and the car park.

Kilve and East Quantoxhead

With the risk of French invasion now passed, you can spy out these Tudor villages and breezy cliffs without fearing arrest.

DISTANCE 3 miles (4.8km)   MINIMUM TIME 1hr 30min

ASCENT/GRADIENT 250ft (76m) ▲▲▲   LEVEL OF DIFFICULTY ✦✦✦

PATHS Tracks, field paths, and grassy cliff top, 4 stiles

LANDSCAPE Tudor villages, farmland and coastline

SUGGESTED MAP OS Explorer 140 Quantock Hills & Bridgwater

START / FINISH Grid reference: ST 144442

DOG FRIENDLINESS Extra care along cliff top, unstable near edge

PARKING Pay-and-display at sea end of Sea Lane

PUBLIC TOILETS At car park (closed October to February)

With two Tudor villages, industrial remnants dating from only a century ago, and a lucid display of geology underfoot, this is a walk to stimulate the brain as well as the lungs.

Jobs for the Priests

The chantry chapel at Kilve is built in the local grey shale, but with the arches picked out in orange Quantock sandstone. The sandstone is easier to work into shaped blocks, but has been eroded by the sea winds. This chantry housed five priests whose sole function was the saying of prayers and masses for the deceased Simon de Furneaux and his family. The doctrine was that the rich could pay their way out of purgatory by setting up such chapels. This created employment for priests, but contributed to the general loss of credibility of the Catholic faith. In fact Kilve Chantry closed even before the Reformation, when a Lollard dissenter married into the family in the late 14th century. Later it was used by smugglers for storing brandy and burnt down around 1850 in an alcohol fire. Behind the ruins, the Chantry House has a pigeon loft still in use.

The old (possibly Saxon) preaching cross in Quantoxhead churchyard is a viewpoint for the Manor House. It also looks on to the back of Quantoxhead Farm, where the semi-circular wing is a horse-gang. This once housed a capstan where horses walked in circles to power, via an endless belt, farm machinery in the main building. The church itself has fossils incorporated into the walls, and Tudor-carved pew ends.

The Spies who Wrote Sonnets

When Samual Taylor Coleridge and William Wordsworth walked here, their particular interest was in the Holford stream. Coleridge planned a poem in his deceptively simple 'conversational' style, tracing the stream from its birth high in Hodder Combe (see Walk 13). However, the two poets had already aroused local suspicions by their comings and goings, and both had been enthusiastic supporters of the French Revolution in its early days. This was 1797: England was in the grip of invasion fever; and Kilve has a small but usable harbour. Accordingly, a government agent called James Walsh was sent to investigate. He quizzed a footman about their dinner-time conversation: it was reported as being quite impossible to understand, which was, of course, most suspicious. The agent followed them to Kilve. Lurking behind a gorse bush, he heard them discussing 'Spy Nosy' and thought he'd been found out. They had actually been talking about the German philosopher, Spinoza... Coleridge never got round to writing his poem *The Brook* – but Wordsworth did. Twenty years later, he adopted his friend's plan into a sequence of sonnets on Lakeland's River Duddon.

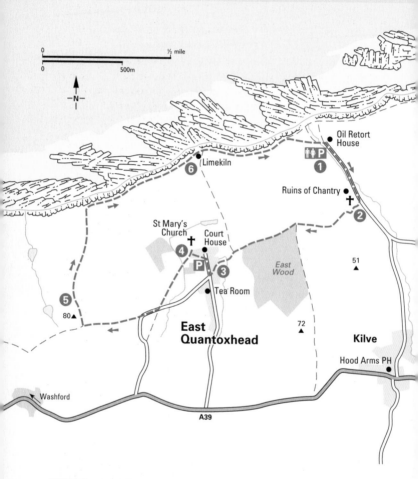

WALK 12 DIRECTIONS

❶ From the car park head back along the lane to the ruined chantry. Turn into the churchyard through a lychgate. Such gates were built to shelter coffins and their bearers: this one is too small for its purpose, so must be a modern reconstruction. Pass to the left of the church, to reach a kissing gate.

❷ A signposted track crosses a field to a gate; bear right to another gate and pass along the foot of East Wood. (At its far end, a stile allows wandering into the wood, from April to August only.) Ignoring the stile on the left, keep ahead to a field gate with a stile and a track crossing a stream.

3 The track bends left past gardens and ponds of East Quantoxhead to reach a tarred lane. Turn right, towards the Tudor Court House, but before its gateway bear left into a car park. Pass through to a tarred path and a kissing gate. In an open field this bears right, to St Mary's Church.

4 Return to the kissing gate but don't go through, instead bear right to a field gate, and cross the field beyond to a distant gate and a lane. Turn right and, where the lane bends left, keep ahead into a green track. At its top, turn right at a 'Permissive path' noticeboard.

5 Follow field-edges, with hedges on your right, down to the cliff top, and turn right. A clifftop path leads to a kissing gate before a sharp dip, with a ruined lime kiln opposite. This was built around 1770 to process limestone, which was shipped from Wales, into lime for the fields and for mortar. The foreshore below the kiln is limestone, but it was still easier to bring it by sea across the Bristol Channel.

6 Turn around the head of the dip, and back left to the cliff top. Here an iron ladder descends to the foreshore: you can see alternating layers of blue-grey lias (a type of limestone) and grey shale. Fossils can be found here, but be aware that the cliffs are unstable – hard hats are now standard wear for geologists. Alternatively, given a suitably trained dog and the right sort of spear, you could pursue the traditional sport of 'glatting' – hunting conger eels in the rock pools. Continue along the wide clifftop path until a tarred path bears off to the right, crossing the stream studied by Coleridge. As you come into the car park, on your left is the brick chimney of a short-lived Oil Retort House (for oil distillation) from 1924; there is oil in the grey shale, but it's proabably less trouble to get it from Texas.

An Amble in the Quantocks

An up-and-down walk in the glorious Quantock combes.

DISTANCE 5.5 miles (8.8km) **MINIMUM TIME** 2hrs 40min

ASCENT/GRADIENT 1000ft (305m) ▲▲▲ **LEVEL OF DIFFICULTY** ✚✚✚

PATHS Wide, smooth paths, with one slightly rough descent, no stiles

LANDSCAPE Deep, wooded hollows and rolling hilltops

SUGGESTED MAP OS Explorer 140 Quantock Hills & Bridgwater

START / FINISH Grid reference: ST 154410

DOG FRIENDLINESS Well-trained dogs can usually remain off lead throughout

PARKING At back of Holford (free)

PUBLIC TOILETS None en route

The great beauty of these hills, says Dorothy Wordsworth, is their wild simplicity. We often hear of the 'Lakes poets', but in fact Coleridge wrote most of his best-known works (*Kubla Khan*, Christabel) while he was living in Somerset, and his neighbour, Wordsworth, started his poetic career here as well. Coleridge was the first to move to the Quantocks, invited by a friendly bookseller, from Nether Stowey, who had noticed a cottage to let at the bottom of his garden. A year later Wordsworth and his sister moved into the rather grand house of Alfoxton (now a hotel).

A Poetic Revolution

This took place in the heady years after the French Revolution, and the ultimate aim of the two friends was to set up a sort of poets' commune, gathering like-minded radicals for a group emigration to America. In the meantime, the two young men revolutionised English poetry. They were key players in the Romantic Revival, overthrowing the stilted formal verse of the previous hundred years, by creating Romantic poetry as a means of describing and expressing strong emotion.

Amazingly, Coleridge's most celebrated work, *The Rime of the Ancient Mariner*, was written in the Quantocks at a time when his entire experience of sea voyaging was a crossing of the Severn by the Chepstow ferry. The poem was roughed out in the course of a walk taken by Coleridge, Wordsworth and Wordsworth's sister, Dorothy. They set out from Alfoxton at 4pm on a November afternoon in 1797; this was timed so that they could watch the dusk give way to moonlight over the Bristol Channel. After crossing the Quantocks they continued by the coast path (see Walk 10), finally arriving at Dulverton four days later. Coleridge's mesmeric Christabel recalls the wooded combes of Holford. *In This Lime-tree Bower My Prison*, Coleridge himself was frustratingly trapped at home in Stowey, after his wife Sara had spilt scalding milk on his foot. Meanwhile, his friends were following your present walk up to Bicknoller Post and enjoying the view over the Bristol Channel from the Quantock Ridge.

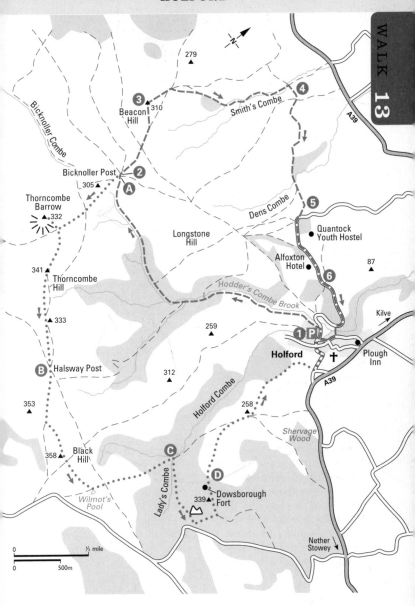

WALK 13 DIRECTIONS

1 Two tracks leave the road beside the car park. Take the right-hand one, which is marked with a bridleway sign. It becomes an earth track through woods, with Hodder's Combe Brook on its right. After 0.75 mile (1.2km) the small track fords the stream

and forks. Take the right-hand option, entering a side valley. The path runs up the valley floor, crossing to the right-hand side of the stream – ignore a further side valley and path forking left. Go up gently through oakwoods floored with bilberry (locally known as 'whortleberry'), then mixed heather and bracken, to reach the

47

Quantock ridge. As the ground eases, keep ahead over two cross-tracks to Bicknoller Post.

2 Just behind the oak post turn right then keep slightly left and uphill on the widest of the tracks. This track becomes a double one, almost a 'dual carriageway'. Bear left off it to the trig point on Beacon Hill.

3 At the trig point bend half right to another marker post on the 'dual carriageway' track. A smaller path goes down directly ahead, into Smith's Combe. The path weaves around, crossing the stream several times.

4 At the foot of the valley, with green fields below, is a 4-way 'Quantock Greenway' signpost: turn right ('Holford'), uphill at first. The path runs around the base of the hills, with a belt of trees below and then the green fields. At the first spur crest is another signpost: keep ahead for Holford. The path runs around the base of the hills, with a belt of trees below and then the green fields. It drops to cross a stream,

Dens Combe. After 0.25 mile (400m) reach a junction with a wide gate leading out on tarmac.

5 Don't go through the gate, but strike uphill to another 'Quantock Greenway' signpost. Keep left to pass above a pink house on to a tarred lane. Follow it ahead below a couple of houses. The lane runs out past Alfoxton, with the walled garden of the grand house (once Wordsworth's, now a hotel) on the left and the stable block with its clock on the right. At the foot of the hotel driveway is a small parking area.

6 Follow the lane for 650yds (594m) then, as it bends right, look out for a waymarker and railings a little way down in the trees. Below is a spectacular footbridge leading across into Holford. Turn right, and at the first junction turn right again, to the car park.

A Quantock Canter

Stretch your legs a little more along the extensive Quantock ridge.

See map and information panel for Walk 13

DISTANCE *7.5 miles (12.1km)*	MINIMUM TIME *3hrs 45min*
ASCENT/GRADIENT *1,500ft (457m)* ▲▲▲	LEVEL OF DIFFICULTY **+++**

WALK 14 DIRECTIONS
(Walk 13 option)

Quantock's long, high-level ridge is an invitation to a longer and more vigorous walk – even if you won't be able to keep up with the horse-riders who find this open heathland ideal for a breezy canter.

From Bicknoller Post, Point **Ⓐ** (Point **②** on Walk 13), keep ahead for 25yds (23m), and turn left on the main track. It skirts to the left of a slight rise, to reach, after 0.25 mile (400m), the head of Bicknoller Combe.

As the main track contours away left, fork right on a track rising ahead into a shallow dip in the skyline. In this wide col, the track bends left (for Thorncombe Hill) but first you can take a diversion to the right to Thorncombe Barrow; its small grassy hump is a fine viewpoint away from the track traffic. Return to the main track and follow it over Thorncombe Hill. The track continues through a slight dip where the bypass track rejoins from the left, and then to the col at Halsway Post, Point **Ⓑ**.

From the oak post, tracks follow a fence up the next rise, and turn left past tumuli to the trig point on Black Hill. Bear left and cross a track on to a wide, green path.

This descends gently to reach a small pond, Wilmot's Pool. Bear left on a rather muddy path. After 200yds (183m) this goes straight across a much wider track. It descends gently into trees, and then more steeply to the stream in Lady's Combe, Point **Ⓒ**.

Cross and turn right, upstream. The path follows the stream for 150yds (137m) then slants uphill, becoming rather steep at the top. At the path's high point, turn left on a wide cross-path to continue uphill. At an earth bank, this path drops ahead, but again turn left to continue uphill into Dowsborough Fort. Some stonework is visible as you enter the fortifications. The path keeps ahead just inside the earth wall. After some wet peaty ground, it turns down right, to leave the rampart, Point **Ⓓ**.

Head straight down the ridge on the wide path, climb slightly to a rise with a cairn, and continue towards Holford, now visible below. The path drops into woodland and reaches a lane with the main A39 close by on the right. Turn left towards Holford. Ignore the first turn-off left, for Holford Combe, and take the second turn-off, signposted to the car park.

River Parrett and Canal

*From Bridgwater walk out beside a river
and back beside a canal.*

DISTANCE 6 miles (9.7km)	**MINIMUM TIME** 2hrs 15min
ASCENT/GRADIENT Negligible ▲▲▲	**LEVEL OF DIFFICULTY** +++

PATHS Broad, made-up paths and a smaller riverside path, 4 stiles

LANDSCAPE Reed beds and tidal riverside, tree-lined tow path

SUGGESTED MAP OS Explorer 140 Quantock Hills & Bridgwater

START / FINISH Grid reference: ST 315359

DOG FRIENDLINESS Off-lead on tow path and most of riverside; no fouling

PARKING Lakeside car park (free) at south-east corner of Bridgwater

PUBLIC TOILETS Blake Park, where A39 crosses River Parrett

WALK 15 DIRECTIONS

Leave the car park back on to the road; turn right, and again right into Plum Lane. Pass houses, with glimpses of the lake on your right. At a cupressus hedge fork left, and after 65yds (60m) keep ahead on path to the side of River Parrett. Turn right to pass under a low arch of a railway bridge, the Somerset Bridge. Cross the attached footbridge, and turn back left under another low arch, well-scratched by motor traffic. Continue upstream on a lane with the River Parrett now on your left. Reed beds and flooded ground are on the right: these

are the excavations of the former Bridgwater Brick and Tile Works. The use of this brick and tile for all of the older buildings gives the town its orangy-brown colouring.

Under the motorway the track turns aside to the right, but continue ahead next to the river. After one open field, a stile leads into the Screech Owl Nature Reserve. The reed beds were once the haunt of the bittern, a bird rather like a small brown heron, that hides in the reeds by pointing its neck and beak vertically upwards, and that has a strange booming cry – but it has not yet returned to Bridgwater. However, the sharp-eyed may spot otter slides running down the mud into the river. At night the otters commute through the town centre to another flooded brickworks at Chilton Trinity. In June and July bird experts will be listening out for the very rare Cetti's warbler.

The path leaves the reserve at a second stile, and continues beside the river on the embankment. It emerges through a broken gate on to a lane. Turn right, crossing the railway by a bridge. As the lane rises again towards a second bridge, this time over the Bridgwater and Taunton Canal, turn right to the tow path.

Head along the wide, smooth path: the canal is on your left, with the Quantock Hills rising in the distance. Swans operate on this stretch, so if you stop to admire the view you may get pestered for your sandwich crusts.

You can also contemplate the traffic arteries of three centuries. In the 1960s the M5 motorway cut journey times between Taunton and London in half. A century before, the railway had reduced the same journey from days to hours. But the coming of the canal, earlier still, had the greatest impact: a single horse could haul the loads of 800 pack-ponies. The 18th-century engineers who oversaw the canal system brought the Industrial Revolution to Bridgwater.

After 0.5 mile (800m) you reach the Boat and Anchor Inn. Its bricks and tiles have moved hardly a 0.25 mile (400m) from their origin in the clay pits behind. Some 50ft (15m) above its chimneypots the traffic zooms past on the M5: damaging, but not managing to destroy, the tranquil canalside scene. As you pass below the road, the sudden perspective of 2,000ft (60m) of concrete bridge piers is, in its way, impressive.

About 0.25 mile (400m) later a small swing bridge crosses the canal at the end of Marsh Lane. Continue with the canal on your right. The tow path passes under the handsome brick arch of Hamp Bridge. Now the river and canal converge, and you can see on the opposite side the sluice where surplus canal water drains into the Parrett. On the left-hand side is a pond with many waterfowl. The tow path passes under a bridge and, after 130yds (118m), a wider one carrying the A38, to join a tarred wide path. Fewer than 20 paces later turn left through a gap to turn right alongside Browne Pond to a tarred path. This rises to cross the canal on another little brick bridge. Where it forks, keep to the right, to arrive at a large crossroads with traffic-lights.

Cross the A39 on your left into Taunton Road. Bear right beside the church to the Blake statue and Cornhill shopping street. Ahead, cross a black-railed bridge over River Parrett, and turn right along Salmon Parade.

Cross the A38 into a riverside lane signed 'Colley Lane Industrial Estate'. After 350yds (320m), opposite a fire station, a concrete ramp leads up to a gravel path alongside the river. Follow it under Somerset Bridge, then retrace your steps to the car park.

Wiveliscombe and the Tone

A pretty village and a wooded riverside on the edge of the Brendons.

DISTANCE 6 miles (9.7km)	**MINIMUM TIME** 3hrs 15min
ASCENT/GRADIENT 1,000ft (300m) ▲▲▲	**LEVEL OF DIFFICULTY** ✦✦✦

PATHS Tracks, a quiet lane, a few field-edges, 2 stiles

LANDSCAPE Wooded river valley and agricultural slopes

SUGGESTED MAP OS Explorer 128 Taunton & Blackdown Hills

START / FINISH Grid reference: ST 080279

DOG FRIENDLINESS On lead in two short field sections and alongside River Tone sections

PARKING North Street, Wiveliscombe

PUBLIC TOILETS At car park

Wiveliscombe formed around a crossroads that was probably more important in the Iron Age than it is today. Its earliest building is the earth fort on Castle Hill. It became quietly prosperous after Edward the Confessor gave the Manor Farm to the Bishop of Bath and Wells in the 11th century. The bishop brought in the latest monastic improvements and set up a small holiday palace for himself. It has remained prosperous ever since.

From Wool Bales to Real Ales

For most of its history Wiveliscombe has lived on wool. In the 18th century it manufactured a rough blue cloth, called Penistones, that clothed the slave population of the West Indies. Today the village has become the real ale capital of Somerset, with two separate breweries established in the late 1970s, making the Exmoor and the Cotleigh Ales. William Hancock began the first Wiveliscombe brewery in 1807. By the 1920s it was the largest brewing operation in the South West, but mergers led to its closure in 1959.

Stable Times

Wiveliscombe is away from the main roads, and also from the tourist trail, and remains largely self-sufficient: a former market town, now a local shopping centre. The town is known affectionately as Wivey, pronounced 'Wivvy'. It has moved peacefully through the centuries, almost untouched by national politics. In the 1670s the town's churchwardens were in trouble for not being nasty enough to Quakers and other nonconformists. Ten years later a survey recorded accommodation available for 76 horses and 53 human beings; the White Hart, the Bear and and the Courtyard Inn are still open for business. In 1804 the National Health Service arrived over 140 years early in the form of a free dispensary for working people and the poor.

WIVELISCOMBE

Architectural Pot-pourri

The buildings of Wiveliscombe are a pick-and-mix of the last 1,000 years. The town hall is, sadly, boarded up; it's Victorian but looks Georgian. Opposite is an absurd building called the Court House. Technically late-Victorian, it belongs to no known architectural style, its overhanging storeys are hung with tiles and decorated with carved animal heads. In the High Street you pass between modest 18th-century terraces; the archway on the right was for stagecoaches, the one on the left may have been part of the bishop's summer palace. South Street was formerly known as 'Gullet', being the way the rainwater ran out of the town. Down in Church Street Nos 10 and 12 are timber-framed medieval cottages: No 10 has some medieval brickwork and No 12 has an upstairs windowsill that's served many centuries. The houses in Rotton Row show the local, plum-coloured sandstone. This has also been used in the 19th-century church near by and throughout the town, giving it a slightly autumnal, bruised look.

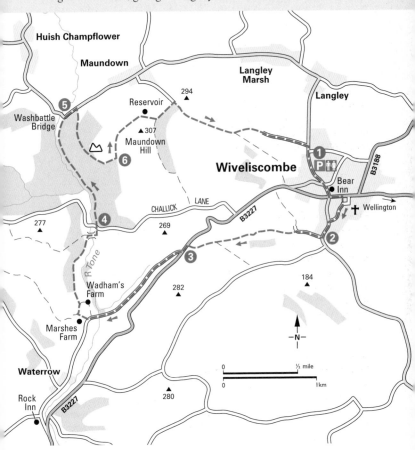

WALK 16 DIRECTIONS

❶ Turn left out of the car park into the Square, head down High Street and turn left at the traffic-lights into Church Street. Turn right, down steps under an arch, to reach Rotton Row. Continue down to South Street and turn left along the pavement past a school.

WALK 16

2 At the end of the village (house No 2) turn right, along a lane, and go ahead through a gate with a footpath sign. Cross the stile ahead, and the bottom edges of three fields. Now the stile in the hedge ahead has grown over, so head up to the left for 30yds (27m) to a gateway before returning to the field foot to pass through a group of farm buildings. Continue in the same direction up the left-hand edge of the field above to reach a gate leading on to the B3227.

WHAT TO LOOK OUT FOR

Look under Washbattle Bridge and you may catch a glimpse of one of our less-known endangered species, the white-clawed crayfish. It's at risk of global extinction because of disease spread by the introduction of signal crayfish.

3 Turn left, then right into a lane heading downhill. After about 0.75 mile (1.2km) it crosses the River Tone and bends left at Marshes Farm. Keep ahead, on a track marked by a bridleway sign. Do not turn right here on the track towards Wadham's Farm but keep uphill to join an upper farm track. Turn right to the top of a deeply sunken lane. Turn right in this, descending towards the farm, but at its first buildings turn left. This track runs up the River Tone. With houses visible ahead, turn right to cross a footbridge and turn left to Challick Lane.

4 The track continues upstream beside the River Tone through very pleasant woodland to reach Washbattle Bridge.

5 Turn right, up the road, for 200yds (183m). A forest

WHERE TO EAT AND DRINK

The Bear Inn, close to the car park, is ancient but unassuming. It serves good bar food, there is a play area for children and well-behaved dogs are welcome. It won an award from CAMRA in 2007, and offers both of the Wivey-brewed real ales.

track, with a footpath signpost, leads uphill on the right. With a pheasant fence alongside, bear left on to a wide path that continues uphill. At the wood edge, exit through a field gate and then turn right, to cross the bottom corner of a field to more woodland opposite. Turn uphill alongside this to reach a gate beside a large concrete water tank.

WHILE YOU'RE THERE

The gardens at Cothay Manor date from 1921 – this is the Sissinghurst 'Vita Sackville-West' style with garden 'rooms' in different colour schemes. They are laid around a medieval manor house (open by appointment). The gardens are open three afternoons a week from spring to autumn. They're rather hard to find, at grid reference ST 085213 between Wiveliscombe and Wellington.

6 Go through this gate and turn left, with a hedge beside you on the left. The next gate opens on to a hedged track. This turns right, and passes a reservoir at the summit of Maundown Hill. At the top of a tarred public road turn sharply right on to a track that becomes a descending, hedged path. At a signposted fork turn left on to a contouring path. Soon a tarred lane leads down into the town, with the car park near by on the right.

Close to the Border at the Back of Blackdown

Stapley's little valley looks down over the county boundary into Devon, towards a grim murder scene.

DISTANCE	3 miles (4.8km) MINIMUM TIME 1hr 40min
ASCENT/GRADIENT	500ft (152m) ▲▲▲ LEVEL OF DIFFICULTY +++
PATHS	Field-edges, and small woodland paths, 14 stiles
LANDSCAPE	Wooded hill slopes
SUGGESTED MAP	OS Explorer 128 Taunton & Blackdown Hills
START / FINISH	Grid reference: ST 188136
DOG FRIENDLINESS	Some freedom in first, woodland, half of walk
PARKING	Small pull-in beside water treatment works at east end of Stapley; verge parking at walk start
PUBLIC TOILETS	None en route; closest at Hemyock

The forests of the Blackdown borders were almost the last part of Somerset to be cleared for agriculture. Here are few proper villages, just the occasional cluster of cottages around a farm. There was no obvious place for the parish church and it stands almost alone at what was once a convenient track junction. With the mechanisation of farming, the area went into decline again.

During the 19th century the population outside the small towns halved. Today a retired couple may occupy a cottage built for a farmworker's family of eight or a dozen people. This quiet corner of the upper Culm Valley was briefly infamous in the 1850s, when a native of this borderland became one of the last Englishmen to be hanged in public.

The Clayhidon Murder

'I think that man gathers more money than anyone else in the parish.' George Sparkes, the speaker, had just received £1 1s 5d, some butter and a drink of beer as his pay for six days of tough fieldwork in the February frost. The man he spoke of, Richard Blackmore, was a local land surveyor who had spent the day collecting tithes and taxes.

Blackmore was carrying £16 in notes and gold sovereigns – about £3,000 in today's money. The two men were drinking in the White Hart at Clayhidon until 1am. Sparkes soon ran out of money. He tried to raise cash at cards, lost, and ended the evening owing Blackmore three pints. Drunk and resentful, he snatched a pair of tongs from the smithy, stalked the rent collector through the fields, and battered him to death. Some of the bloodstained sovereigns were found in his cottage the next morning.

Measures of Humanity

The trial, which took place at Exeter, was not a long one. Sparkes seemed as shocked as anyone at what he had done; but the law allowed only one sentence. It's clear that the judge was reluctant to pronounce it for so senseless a crime: he voiced the words 'to be hanged by the neck until dead' almost inaudibly, and bowed his head in tears. It is said that 10,000 people attended the hanging. The reporter for the *Exeter Flying Post* (April 1853) recorded disapprovingly the presence of women and children: 'the broadcloth of the middle classes jostling the cotton of the mechanics and labourers – a strange motley for so sad a scene and too painfully indicative of the fact that the 'lower orders' are not the only people who relish the sight of a public strangulation'.

The gallows employed the 'new drop' – a humane innovation so that the condemned man should break his neck in the fall. And the space below the trapdoor was boarded in, allowing him to die in private. The White Horse Inn has gone, but there's a memorial stone at the murder site – this is just south of of Clayhidon, at the foot of Battle Street.

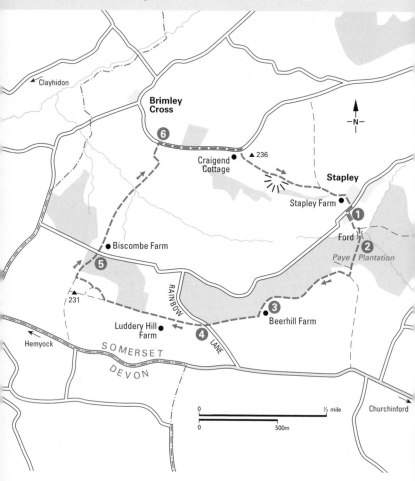

WALK 17 DIRECTIONS

❶ A phone box currently marks the start of the walk. Some 20 paces below it a lane runs down between houses. After 100yds

(91m) keep ahead into a shady path. At a stile bear right to a ford with a footbridge.

❷ Head up a wide track. At a junction cross on to a small,

waymarked path that's muddy to start with. This heads uphill, following a bank, to a stile. In the field beyond (abundant nettles in season) bear right, to a field corner and a stile back into woodland. A small path runs along the top edge of Paye Plantation, to emerge near Beerhill Farm.

WHERE TO EAT AND DRINK

The York Inn at Churchinford is a typical country hotel, with hanging baskets at the door and 15th-century beams above the open fire. Dogs are welcome (bar only), also children (restaurant only). Alternatively, you can cross into Devon to visit the murder site and a classic country pub with good food and a view, the Half Moon at Clayhidon.

3 Bear left for 100yds (91m) to a waymarked gate below the farm, and a second just beyond. Keep ahead, below the farm and above the wood, to a gate with cattle trough. In the field beyond, follow the top edge of the wood to Rainbow Lane.

4 Cross the lane to a signposted stile. Pass along the left edge of a long narrow field. Flinty-looking chert lies in the field, and over on the left, Luddery Hill Farm is built of it. After this field, a stile leads into ash trees. Again the path runs along the top edge of the wood.

WHILE YOU'RE THERE

Churchstanton church has a charming setting and many interesting features. The youngest members of the party will particularly appreciate one gargoyle (the south west one on the tower). Less charming are the village stocks, of various sizes, preserved in the church porch.

With an isolated house visible ahead, a waymarker indicates the diverted right of way bearing right. This path slants gently downhill, to meet the house's driveway at a bend. Cross on to a wide path just above the driveway. At the end of the wood turn down right, to rejoin the driveway to the road below.

5 Cross into the trackway of Biscombe Farm. Bear left to a field gate, and go down the right edge of a large field to a stile in a hedge gap on the right. Slant down the following field to a stile at its bottom, right-hand corner, with stepping stones across the stream beyond. Go up the right-hand edge of the next field to a stile. This leads into a sunken track; turn left and follow it up to a lane. (If the track is impossibly soggy, you can turn left along the field top and through a gate to join it higher up.)

6 Turn right to walk up the road. Where the road levels and bends left, turn right into the driveway of Craigend Cottage to find a stile where the driveway bends right. Turn left along field tops, with a hedge bank on your left and a view of Devon over your right shoulder. At the end of a second field a field gate leads to a tractor track. After a short, muddy passage past Stapley Farm you reach the village road at the phone box.

WHAT TO LOOK OUT FOR

The whitish, shiny stone found in field walls and in Luddery Hill Farm is chert. It looks like flint, but unlike flint it comes in chunks rather than rounded nodules. The toughness of chert is one reason why the Blackdown Hills exist at all.

A Walk in Prior's Park Woodlands

Prior's Park Wood is at its best with autumn's colours or spring's bluebells beautifully concealing some intricate geology.

DISTANCE 5 miles (8km)	MINIMUM TIME 2hrs 40min
ASCENT/GRADIENT 700ft (213m) ▲▲▲	LEVEL OF DIFFICULTY ✦✦✦

PATHS Rugged in Prior's Park Wood, otherwise comfortable, 7 stiles

LANDSCAPE Steep, wooded slopes

SUGGESTED MAP OS Explorer 128 Taunton & Blackdown Hills

START / FINISH Grid reference: ST 211182

DOG FRIENDLINESS Mostly open woodland

PARKING Roadside pull-off between post office and Blagdon Inn

PUBLIC TOILETS None en route

Somerset is a landscape of hills that are small but steep-sided. There's a reason for this particular formation. The rocks that are now Somerset did not form until after Britain's main mountain-building episode, the collision of Scotland with England. Since then the county has been gently lifted (by the 'Africa Crunch'), but never seriously crumpled and mashed. Its rocks still lie fairly flat.

The shape of this landscape is inextricably linked to the development of the underlying rocks. If a layer of tough rock lays fairly flat on top of much softer rocks, then where the tough rock is worn away, so the softer rocks, too, will quickly disappear. And so we end up with a flat-topped hill with a distinctive sudden edge. Such hills – at Ham Hill, at Cadbury or at Dolebury in the Mendips – proved particularly convenient for building Iron Age forts on. The harder rock on top may be limestone – as at Glastonbury – or the greensand of the Blackdown Hills, which features on this walk.

Goyals

Small streams, such as the Curdleigh Brook seen on this walk, cut into the hard plateau rock of the Blackdown Hills, forming the little tree-lined valleys that are so typically Somerset that there's even a special Somerset word for them. 'When little boys laughed at me at Tiverton, for talking about a 'Goyal', a big boy clouted them on the head, and said that it was in Homer, and meant the hollow of the hand'; explained Jan Ridd of Exmoor, the hero of *Lorna Doone*. 'Still I know what it means well enough – to wit, a long trough among wild hills, falling towards the plain country, rounded at the bottom, perhaps, and stiff, more than steep, at the sides of it'. R D Blackmore's fictional Somerset man certainly understood the character of his county's topography.

Blackdown Hills

Standing on the plateau of the Blackdown Hills, you gaze across the wide vale of Taunton at the Quantocks and Brendons. It is not too hard to see the plateau of Blackdown and the plateau of the Brendons as being part of the same ground. Indeed, this is a former ground level of 40 million years ago. But what force or process has carried away the 10 miles (16.1km) of scenery that lay in between?

If all the high ground above Taunton Deane had been carried away in goyles, Blackdown should have a ragged edge rather than the straight one we see. All credit to the 19th-century geologist Sir Henry de la Beche, not for solving the problem, but for seeing that there was one to be solved. The answer lies in a process called solufluction. It still goes on today in the tundras of Alaska. In the brief, Ice-Age summer a soggy mixture of half-melted soil and slush can slip downhill over the frozen ground below. Such landslips can still be detected on the northern slopes of the Blackdown Hills, as well as in the Quantocks. They may represent the most important process which shaped today's Somerset.

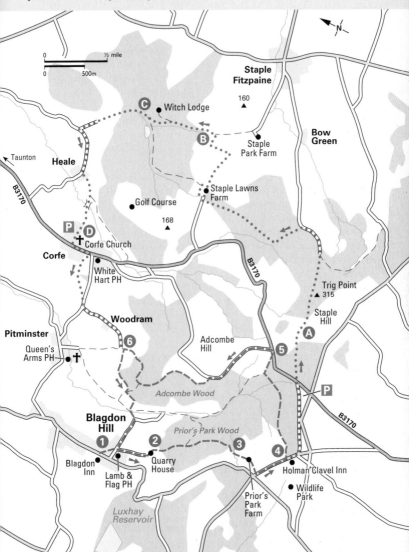

WALK 18 DIRECTIONS

❶ The walk starts at the phone box opposite the Blagdon Inn. Cross a stile and follow the left edge of a triangular field to another stile into Curdleigh Lane. Cross into the ascending Quarry Lane. Pass between the buildings of Quarry House, on to a track running ahead up into and through Prior's Park Wood.

❷ From mid-April this wood is a delight with wild garlic and foxtail grass (actually a sedge). The track is also fine (but possibly muddy) in autumn. Keep uphill, ignoring a side-path left. The main path eventually declines into a muddy trod, slanting up and leftwards to a small gate at the top of the wood.

❸ Pass along the wood's top edge to a gate. Cross the next field between fences to Prior's Park Farm, passing between its buildings to its access track and a road. Turn left and follow the road with care, as it's a fairly fast section, towards the Holman Clavel Inn.

❹ Just before the inn turn left on to a forest track. Where the track ends a small path runs ahead, zig-zagging down before crossing a stream. At the wood's edge

WHAT TO LOOK OUT FOR

If undertaking this walk in springtime, a wild flower identification book might be helpful as there are many unusual woodland plants en route. The early purple orchid (flowering in early June) is one to look out for.

turn right to walk up a wider path to reach the B3170.

❺ At once turn left on the lane signed 'Feltham'. After 0.5 mile (800m) a wide gateway on the left leads to an earth track. This runs along the top of Adcombe Wood for 0.5 mile (800m), then down inside it. Once below the wood follow the track downhill for 180yds (165m). Look for a gate with a signpost on the left-hand side and go through it.

❻ Follow the hedge on the right to a stile and footbridge, then bend left, below the foot of the wood, to another stile. Ignore a stile into the wood on the left, but continue along the wood's foot to the next field corner. Here a further stile enters the wood but turn right, beside the hedge, to a tarmac track. Turn left, then bear right along – Curdleigh Lane, back into Blagdon Hill.

WHERE TO EAT AND DRINK

Blagdon Inn is a charming 17th-century inn serving good food and real ales. Blagdon Hill also has the cheerful Lamb & Flag, which has a beer garden and welcomes children, while half-way round the walk is the Holman Clavel Inn. Those taking Walk 19, the longer option, can find refuge in the attractive inns at Corfe (the White Hart) and Pitminster (the Queen's Arms).

WHILE YOU'RE THERE

The Museum of Somerset (reopens Summer 2010) in Taunton Castle. This was the principal site of the `Bloody Assizes'. About 500 Monmouth rebels were put on trial here: 200 of them were executed in the surrounding streets and most of the rest were transported into slavery in the West Indies. Several of their ghosts are said to haunt the building. It also houses an Iron Age canoe which was unearthed near Glastonbury.

Blackdown Heights

An attractive longer walk to the Blackdown's highest points.

See map and information panel for Walk 18

DISTANCE *9.25 miles (14.9km)*   **MINIMUM TIME** *4hrs 30min*

ASCENT/GRADIENT *1,000ft (305m)* ▲▲▲   **LEVEL OF DIFFICULTY** +++

START / FINISH *Grid reference: ST 211182*

PARKING *Roadside pull-off between post office and Blagdon Inn*

WALK 19 DIRECTIONS
(Walk 18 option)

Follow Walk 18 past Point ❹ to Holman Clavel Inn. Above the inn bear left, then keep ahead on to a minor road. At its end, cross the B3170 to a small gate. A path runs slightly left into a gap in pine woods. From a gate at a fence corner, a path runs ahead through scrub, with a fence nearby on your right, to two field gates. Take the right-hand one, and follow a field's left edge to join a track into woods, Point ❹.

From here to Point ❸, follow waymarkers 'Herepath'. At the track's high point, the trig point of Staple Hill is hidden in woods on the right. Follow the track down to a lane. At its first right bend, take a woodland track on the left signposted 'Wych Lodge Woods'. After 1 mile (1.6km), it emerges at a gate above Staple Park Farm, Point ❸.

Follow waymarks right, left, and right past the farm to a small gate into a large field. Head down its right-hand side to a small gate. Through this, turn left along the top of a field, and at its corner turn right for 150yds (137m) to a narrow gate. Keep to left of a hedge ahead to the next gate, which leads to a woodland track. This runs downhill to join the gravel access track for Witch Lodge. Follow it ahead, downhill, until it doubles back left. Here keep ahead on a downhill path, Point ❸.

The path leads into a track ahead that's rough, then tarred, down to a lane. Turn left for 700yds (640m) to Heale. After a pink house, turn left along a cul-de-sac to the gate at its end. Follow the right edge of the field beyond, with a wiggle to left to a vee-stile. Turn half-right to a stile that leads to a high footbridge hidden in the hedge. Turn left to a kissing gate, with a path leading forward to Corfe Church, Point ❹.

Turn left through Corfe to a field path on the right before a long hedge. Follow the hedge on the right until it turns away, then bear left to a line of oaks. Turn left around the next field's edge, to pass alongside a lane and then join it at the edge of Pitminster. Here a narrow side-lane runs uphill between hedges past Woodram. At its top, ignore a hedged path down right, but keep uphill for another 45yds (40m) to a gate on the right with footpath signpost, Point ❻ of Walk 18.

Over the Edge to Sedgemoor

*From Curry Rivel to the Cider Monument
for a view over the moors.*

DISTANCE 4 miles (6.4km)	**MINIMUM TIME** 1hr 45min

ASCENT/GRADIENT 350ft (107m) ▲▲▲ **LEVEL OF DIFFICULTY** +++

PATHS Paths, tracks and field-edges, 8 stiles

LANDSCAPE Wooded scarp, gentle farmland

SUGGESTED MAP OS Explorer 128 Taunton & Blackdown Hills

START / FINISH Grid reference: ST 391252

DOG FRIENDLINESS Mostly on lead – enclosed pasture and lanes

PARKING Car park at village centre

PUBLIC TOILETS None en route

WALK 20 DIRECTIONS

Curry Rivel is a fairly typical Somerset village, with its mixture of small shops, pubs and stone houses, with the church rising above the tiled rooftops. Modern estates around the village have tried to blend in by using traditional building materials – and perhaps with another couple of centuries of weathering they will. 'Curry' is from the Celtic 'crwy', meaning boundary; 'Rivel' is pronounced like the end of 'arrival' and is the name of the 12th-century feudal overlord Sir Richard Revel.

Head back from the car park to turn right along A378 (Taunton direction). In 110 yds (100m), just after the post office is a high-walled path on the right. At its end turn left, in front of a trimmed yew hedge. Follow the right-hand edge of the field beyond, and cross a driveway to a stile ahead. Just after this stile the tall Pynsent Monument comes into sight on the right: a 140ft (43m) waymark for the next part of your walk.

It was designed by 'Capability' Brown and commemorates an act of 18th-century political sleaze. Sir William Pynsent lobbied the Prime Minister, Pitt the Elder, on behalf of the cider industry. Pitt refrained from raising the duty on cider and in gratitude Pynsent left to Pitt in his will the Burton Pynsent estate. At the time this was a perfectly respectable proceeding, and Pitt raised the column to celebrate it.

Continue always in the same direction, with a fence on your left, to a kissing gate on the left and a lane. Turn right for 170yds (155m) to a gateway with stone pillars. Turn left into a field, and follow its edge round to the right to a kissing gate and the Pynsent Monument with its sudden view ahead over West Sedgemoor.

In July 1685 the Earl of Feversham was sent to crush the Monmouth Rebellion. He chose a camp down in that watery moorland, well-protected by the many rhynes (drainage ditches). Outnumbered and outgunned, Monmouth staked all on a surprise attack. In mist, at dead of night, his pitchfork army crept out of Bridgwater. Each man carried a knife, with orders quietly to stab to death the man next to him if he made a sound. However, a shot was fired – either by accident or treachery. Feversham surrounded the rebels among the rhynes. Some 200 were killed outright (against the King's 16), and in the aftermath many hundreds more were hanged from the signboards of nearby inns.

Pass the monument into a dip, to find a stile at the top corner of open beech wood. A path leads down through the open wood (non-native conifers have been felled here, hence the spindly appearance of the remaining beech and ash trees). At the bottom turn left, just inside the wood, for 275yds (251m) to a stile on the right. Cross open parkland, just to the left of a pond, to a distant gate. This leads back into Burton

Wood. Turn left, on a tarmac track that climbs out of the woods. Some 100yds (91m) later comes a stile on the right; bear slightly left across the field to a stile in the hedge to the A378. Cross into Moortown Lane. This jinks right then left to pass an orchard. It then repeats the manoeuvre, jinking right then left to pass a second orchard. Here you may notice mistletoe in the apple branches. This parasitic plant feeds on the sap of other trees.

Straight after this second orchard turn left through a gate. With a wide, flat view to your right, cross the top edges of two fields, to a green track. Here grows a plant with the divided leaves of the elder, the berries of the elder, but clearly not the elder as it's herbaceous, dying back in winter, unlike a tree. It's the fairly uncommon Danewort. The track emerges on to Holden's Way. Turn left, uphill, ignoring a side road on the right. In another 220yds (201m) take a hole in the hedge on the right, signed 'Williton'. Follow a field-edge to a grey house with pink edges. Pass to its left, to a gap in a tall Cupressus hedge. An enclosed path leads out to the B3168.

Turn left along the pavement, then take the first left into Stoney Lane. Opposite the turn-off is Old Father Time set on a high wall above a letter box. After 180yds (165m) take a street on the right just after wisteria-covered Cross Cottage – it leads back to Curry Rivel's main street.

Ilminster, the River Isle and a Walk in the Woods

A pleasing riverside ramble, an ancient village, and a wood that aspires to being ancient.

DISTANCE 5.75 miles (9.2km)	MINIMUM TIME 2hrs 40min
ASCENT/GRADIENT 500ft (152m) ▲▲▲	LEVEL OF DIFFICULTY ✦✦✦

PATHS *Tracks, wide paths, and riverside field-edges, 4 stiles*

LANDSCAPE *Riverside, and a small wooded hill*

SUGGESTED MAP *OS Explorer 128: Taunton & Blackdown Hills*

START / FINISH *Grid reference: ST 361146*

DOG FRIENDLINESS *Mostly on lead*

PARKING *Wharfe Lane pay-and-display, off Canal Way; or West Street; or by Donyatt Church, Point ⑤*

PUBLIC TOILETS *Ditton Street, signed from the Market Square (walk start)*

These days, nothing in the countryside just happens naturally. Fields are managed for food, although that is starting to change. Woodlands are managed to save valuable wildlife habitats. In the early Middle Ages forests were managed for deer, and for the men (in particular, the King) who hunted the deer. A couple of centuries later, woodlands were for pigs.

The Natural Heritage Age

Today, woods are for natural heritage. At the top of the list, this means mammals (apart from the grey squirrel, a 'baddie'), and birds. Slightly further down come butterflies, followed by woodlice, lichens and the rarer sorts of wild flowers. You don't often hear of woodlands (as opposed to commercial timber forests) being managed for the sake of the trees – perhaps that just sounds too circular. But trees too have their league table. The 'aristocrats' who can trace their lineage back to the ice age – oak, beech, hedge maple – are 'good'. The exception is the sycamore: the sycamore is too good at surviving, and so is considered a weed, to be eradicated. The latecomers, and other ones people may have had a hand in, are intruders; walnut and sweet chestnut are to be controlled or rooted out.

The Dog Age

Towards the bottom of the list comes the naturalist. And still important, but perhaps less so than any of the others, is the ordinary human being: the child looking for conkers, the young couple looking for privacy, the painter or photographer looking for shades of green in dappled sun, those special qualities of woodland light. I don't disagree with this: the oak and the beech are indeed handsome trees, and the spruce is gloomy. Almost all walkers are interested in wildlife. Still, why is the badger a hero but the fox a dubious character? And is it possible that, in another century or two, woodland will be managed mainly for the sake of its most enthusiastic users – our dogs? The first priorities would therefore be big piles of leaves, things that run away, and things that smell interesting when dead.

Herne Hill Wood

Assuming, then, that you're a person with an interest in wildlife (rather than a dog that just wants to chase it), in Herne Hill Wood you might spot: hazel nuts with tiny holes nibbled in them by dormice ('good!'); tree bark chewed away by the grey squirrels ('bad!'); one or two of the squirrels themselves; and you may notice the ferretty smell of badgers. Herne Hill itself was given to the people of Ilminster in 1931. Another four or five centuries should see it turning into a proper 'ancient woodland'.

WALK 21

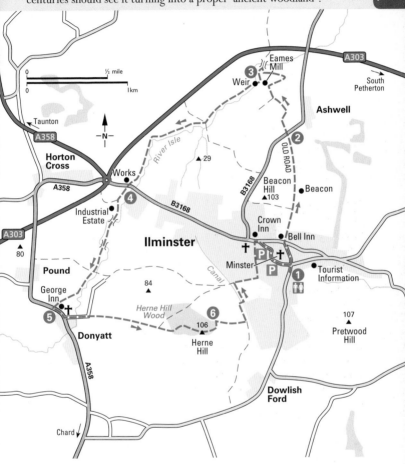

WALK 21 DIRECTIONS

❶ From the Market Square head uphill on North Street. With the ancient Bell Inn on the left, the route continues on a path (Old Road). It rises past communications equipment ancient and modern – a beacon fire-basket and then a mobile phone mast – before descending to the B3168.

❷ Cross with care into a hedged byway to Eames Mill. Turn right, along the waymarked access track. After 220yds (201m) a concrete track turns sharply back left. Just before a bridge, go through a chain gate to follow the River Isle upstream. You have covered 0.25 mile (400m) to pass from the front of Eames Mill to the back, but the rights of way don't allow a more straightforward route.

WALK 21

③ Cross a weir to head upstream with the river on your left. After a mile (1.6km), and ignoring a couple of bridges over the river, you will reach Powrmatic works car park, and a chain gate to the B3168 beyond.

④ Cross the B3168 and then follow a track signed 'Rose Mills Industrial Estate'. Pass along the river bank to the left of the buildings, and then between piles of ironwork and round to right of a large white shed to a footbridge

left alongside the field fence to reach a gate on the right.

⑥ A wide path runs towards Ilminster, with sports fields below. Turn left, between the sports fields and the town, for 200yds (183m) to a yellow litter bin and a green shed. A gap on the right leads to a path alongside a murky remnant of the Chard-Taunton Canal. The slope you just descended was an incline, where barges were hauled on trolleys before the canal continued at a higher level, into a tunnel. Turn right behind tennis courts, and after 250yds (229m) turn left into Abbots Close and on to a tarred path. This leads to West Street, arriving at the Crown Inn. Turn right and bear right into Silver Street, to reach the town centre and the car park.

back into the real world. Now with the river on your right, head upstream in a fenced way to re-cross the river another footbridge. Continue crossing over stiles along the right-hand bank. With the tower of Donyatt church ahead of you, cross diagonally right to a gate by a thatched cottage on to the road.

⑤ Turn left through the village, and bear left past the church. Head straight up Herne Hill as the lane leads to a track, then a field-edge path, then an earth path through Herne Hill Wood. The summit is under tall beeches. A wide avenue ahead leads to a field corner. Continue just inside the wood, passing a bench and trig point on your right, and going down to the wood's foot. Keep right, to the very corner of the wood, before a path bends back

In Praise of Lambrook's Apples

A gentle, secluded ramble around the fields and fragrant apple orchards of central Somerset.

DISTANCE 4.75 miles (7.7km)	**MINIMUM TIME** 2hrs 30min
ASCENT/GRADIENT 350ft (107m) ▲▲▲	**LEVEL OF DIFFICULTY** ✦✦✦

PATHS Little-used field paths (some possibly overgrown by late summer), 25 stiles

LANDSCAPE Fields, orchards, and a little hill

SUGGESTED MAP OS Explorer 129 Yeovil & Sherborne

START / FINISH Grid reference: ST 431190

DOG FRIENDLINESS Even the fiercest dog can't harm an apple tree!

PARKING Street parking in East Lambrook village

PUBLIC TOILETS None en route; nearest at Martock Roundabout on A303

Apples were brought to Somerset by the Romans and caught on immediately. As early as the Arthur legends, Isle Avalon (Glastonbury) is the place of apples. Ten centuries later, the Normans brought the cider idea from northern France. However, even the most traditional of Somerset ciders isn't at all like the light, sparkling drink of Normandy. The real Somerset cider, known as 'scrumpy', is dark and even yeasty, lacks bubbles, and takes a bit of time to get to know. (In this it may perhaps resemble the Somerset cider drinker…)

Sheep's Nose and Brown Snout

Grape juice is already a balanced food for the yeasts of fermentation, and so is the boiled malt extract that makes beer. Squashed apples, however, are not. Sugar is needed for fermentation; tannin gives the sharpness that distinguishes real drinks from alco-pops. Sugar and tannin aren't found in the same apple, so a mixture of sweet, bitter-sweet and bitter-sour varieties is required. As many as 40 different apple varieties can go into the recipe for just one cider. Wonderful names have been given to these ancient cider apples: Tom Putt and Sheep's Nose have been recovered by the National Trust, while varieties such as Kingston Black, Yarlington Mill and Brown Snout have never gone out of favour.

Dead Rat Trick

And then, the yeast needs nitrogen, and apples don't have it. An early trick was to drop a dead rat into the cider barrel – when the rat had completely dissolved, the cider was fit to drink. (Well, obviously not fit to drink before the rat had gone…) Producers of 'real cider' won't stoop to the chemical equivalent of a rat – ammonium sulphate – so fermentation is always chancy. Even so, in spring the orchards are white with blossom from Porlock to Glastonbury. And autumn sees trailer-loads of Stokes Red and Taunton Black holding up the A303 on their way to the cider works at Shepton Mallet (smelled on Walk 35).

EAST LAMBROOK

Like many in this part of the county, the view from Burrow Hill belies its low altitude – a mere 252ft (77m). To the south you look across a patchwork of orchards and pasture. Northwards the land drops away suddenly to the Somerset Levels. Sunset gleams in ripe-apple colours in a hundred rhynes and bits of river – even more spectacular in winter, when much of the country is flooded. Beyond the Levels, the Currys ridge rises – and here too we're looking at cider. The monument at Curry Rivel (see Walk 20) commemorates some parliamentary lobbying by the apple-squashers. The distillers had less reason to be grateful. The industry was taxed to death in the 18th century for the benefit of the London gin trade. The cider trade has recently been reborn – sample the goods at Burrow Hill.

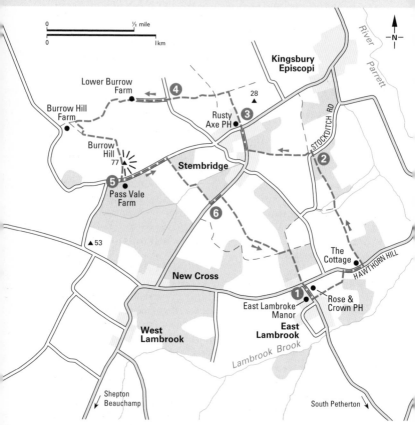

WALK 22 DIRECTIONS

❶ From the village centre crossroads, head south, signposted 'South Petherton', past the Rose & Crown and East Lambrook Manor gardens, then turn left on a track. After one field a track leads left to a lane (Hawthorn Hill). Turn right to The Cottage, where a gate with a stile leads into an orchard on the left. Follow its left edge and the following field. Cross the next field, keeping 70yds (64m) from its left edge, to a gate. Bear right to a stile-with-footbridge and the left edge of another orchard, then take a gateway to follow a hedge between two more orchards. At the end a gate leads on to Stockditch Road.

❷ Turn left for 40yds (37m), on to an overgrown track. From its end the edge of another orchard leads to two stiles and a footbridge. Follow the left-hand edges of two fields to a road, and turn right for 220yds (201m) to the Rusty Axe pub.

❸ Keep ahead, on a track that's tarred at first, past houses. After crossing the crest, the main track turns left. As it bends left again, keep ahead along the field-top hedge (ignoring a waymarker for a different path). Half-way along the hedge, cross two stiles (can be very muddy) into a long field. At its far end, stiles and small gates lead to the left of a house to join a quiet country lane. Turn left a couple of steps to a T-junction then turn right to pass houses.

❹ Follow the lane to Lower Burrow Farm, and follow waymarkers which skirt around the farm buildings to the right. Once through a gate to the right of a large grey shed, bear left,

slanting uphill, to a gateway. Contour across the next field to a double stile. In the next field bear right across it to a gate. Burrow Hill Farm is now just one field ahead. Turn left, up the side of this field and across its top to a gate. Go up the fields above to reach a row of poplars and the summit of Burrow Hill.

❺ Drop down to cross a stile into the lane at Pass Vale Farm and then turn left for 0.25 mile (400m) to a waymarked field gate on the right. (A stile is in the hedge opposite this gate.) Follow the left edges of two fields to a gateway and stile on the left. Continue beside a stream to a brambly stile and turn right to a lane.

❻ Turn left to a double metal gate on the right, opposite a school sign. Follow the left edges of three fields, then bear left over a stile and footbridge to a second bridge just beyond. In the next large field, head diagonally right to the furthest corner. Ignoring a track on the right, take the hedged path ahead, to arrive in a mistletoe orchard. Don't take the obvious gate ahead, heading out of the orchard, but turn right, to its far end, where a lane leads back into East Lambrook.

Golden Stone on the Top of Ham Hill

Ascending the hill whose warm-coloured limestone forms the towns and villages of Somerset.

DISTANCE 4 miles (6.4km)	**MINIMUM TIME** 2hrs
ASCENT/GRADIENT 700ft (213m) ▲▲▲	**LEVEL OF DIFFICULTY** +++

PATHS Well-trodden and sometimes muddy, 2 stiles

LANDSCAPE Steep-sided, wooded hill

SUGGESTED MAP OS Explorer 129 Yeovil & Sherborne

START / FINISH Grid reference: ST 478167

DOG FRIENDLINESS Dogs under control welcome on Ham Hill itself, may need lead elsewhere

PARKING View Point car park on western escarpment of Ham Hill

PUBLIC TOILETS At Ranger Hut near start, and at Stoke Sub Hamden

The yellow limestone, known as Hamstone, found on Ham Hill and nearby Chiseldon is of a local and special sort. Most limestone is formed of sea shells underwater, but Ham Hill was once a wave-battered, shingly bank. These well-broken shell fragments were cemented together, and stained yellow by a seepage of iron oxide, or common rust.

Consequently, the Ham Hill limestone doesn't have intact fossils. More importantly, it doesn't have the crumbliness of most limestones, or the tendency to split apart into layers. It's what is called 'freestone' – it can be worked smooth and carved in any direction. Shaping Hamstone is like cutting cheese rather than flaky pastry.

Romans in the Stone

Traces of early quarrying naturally get dug up and carried away by later quarrying. However, we do know that the Romans quarried here: a Roman coffin made of Ham Hill stone is in the museum at Dorchester. However, it was much later, in the Middle Ages, that the quarries became the making of Somerset – literally. The more important buildings – Montacute House at the foot of the hill, but also Sherborne Abbey, Wells Cathedral and many manor houses – were built of Hamstone throughout.

Shop Local

Because of the cost of hauling the stones, in the days before real roads, buildings such as parish churches used the local stone for masonry but Hamstone for the corners and the tricky bits round the windows. The Yeo and the Parrett provided river transport, and Hamstone could be floated up the Tone to Taunton and Wellington. All over Somerset it's a golden thread running through the richly varied building fabric. Another quality of Hamstone is apparent at Bath, where they had their own sort of freestone and didn't need to use it. The Bathstone, an oolitic limestone, is crumbling in today's polluted atmosphere. The Hamstone, a sort of natural concrete, is more robust. The quarries were worked by hand, using wedges and a type of pick called a 'jadd'. The tremendous labour of lifting the rough-shaped blocks out of the quarries was a spur to ingenuity and mechanical contrivance. Steam-powered cranes came to Ham Hill in the 18th century but, even so, the work was dangerous, with quarrymen injured or crushed to death every year.

Back to the Future

Today two of the quarries have re-opened. They are being worked in the traditional way, with wedges and hand tools. The fork-lift truck provides a safer alternative to the block-and-tackle or steam crane. The stone goes for restoration work and also for new building. Cheap transport in the 20th century meant stone for a fancy façade could come from Spain or even China, but today planners are realising that the local stone is crucial to Somerset's character and charm.

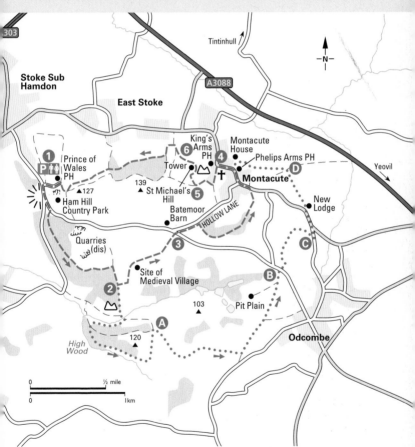

WALK 23 DIRECTIONS

❶ Turn right out of the car park (so that the big, westward view is on the right) to a road junction. Keep left for 35yds (32m) then take a path on the right, signed 'Norton Sub Hamdon'. This leads through woods around the side of Ham Hill, keeping at the same level, around the rim and then just below it, all the way round. When

HAM HILL

WALK 23

WHERE TO EAT AND DRINK

The Prince of Wales, Ham Hill, is a walker's pub. It welcomes dogs and muddy boots. The view over half of Somerset is just as good to sit at with a drink as it is to walk past. The pub is closed on Mondays off-season. Montacute has two attractive old inns, the Phelips Arms and the King's Arms.

open field appears ahead, the path turns right, downhill.

2 Ignore a first gate on the left but go down through a second. Descend grassland into a small valley with the hummocks of the medieval village of Witcombe. Head left up the valley floor, passing to the left of a willow clump. A grassy path slants up the right-hand side of the valley to a field corner. Here turn left on a track that leads to a lane near Batemoor Barn.

3 Hollow Lane descends directly opposite. A gate and gap just to its right lets you pass along the field-edges, then into a wood. Just inside the wood, turn right up steps. A clear path runs just below the top of the wood, then down to the edge of Montacute village. Turn left to pass the entrance to Montacute House, to reach the King's Arms pub.

4 Turn left, past the church; after a duck pond turn right on a permissive path. A kissing gate leads to the base of St Michael's Hill. Turn left for 150yds (137m) to a stile into the woods.

5 The path ahead is arduous. For a gentler way up the hill, turn left around its base to the gateway and stile at the foot of the descending track. Otherwise cross the stile to a very steep path, to the summit tower. The tower is open and its spiral staircase is well worth the climb. Descend the winding main track to the gateway and stile at the hill's foot.

6 Turn half-right and go straight down the field to a gate at its bottom corner. This leads on to a track corner. Turn left and follow the track round the field corner. After 90yds (82m) take a right fork. The earth track runs close to the foot of the woods, passing the ruins of a pump house, and diminishing to a path; it then climbs steps to join a higher one. Turn right to continue close to the foot of the woods until the path emerges at a gate after 500yds (457m). Steps lead up to the Prince of Wales pub. Turn left along its lane, through the hummocks of former quarries, to the car park.

WHAT TO LOOK OUT FOR

The outdoor tables of the Prince of Wales give a clear view of medieval strip lynchets on the hillside. Where valley bottoms were boggy, the well-drained hill slopes were best for cultivation. Strip lynchets were a system of terracing so that at least part of the slope would be gentle enough to cultivate.

WHILE YOU'RE THERE

Montacute House is one of the finest Elizabethan houses in England. There is a back view on Walk 24; this may well tempt you to pay the National Trust's entry fee to get a proper look. Nearby Tintinhull (also National Trust) has a much more modest house in a small but intensely colourful garden.

Ham and Odcombe

*A longer ramble, adding High Wood
to Ham Hill with unexpected views
of Montacute House.*

See map and information panel for Walk 23

DISTANCE *6.5 miles (10.4km)* MINIMUM TIME *3hrs 15min*
ASCENT/GRADIENT *800ft (244m)* ▲▲▲ LEVEL OF DIFFICULTY ✦✦✦

WALK 24 DIRECTIONS
(Walk 23 option)

At Point ❷ of the previous walk follow the fairly steep path down just inside the wood to reach a track below. Cross to a kissing gate and bear right to a gate into High Wood. Bear right on a path that becomes a melancholic laurel tunnel (slightly similar to cloud forests in the Canary Islands) as it works its way round the hill. After 0.25 mile (400m) ignore waymarked side-paths down right and up left. The path works its way right round the hill to emerge into an open field. Keep ahead for 40yds (37m) to rough track and follow it up left, over the end of the hill and down to a kissing gate on the right. Just below is the track crossed earlier, now rejoined at Point ❹.

Turn right for 0.75 mile (1.2km) to a T-junction near a road. Turn left and after 0.25 mile (400m) keep ahead rather than forking right into Odcombe. The track joins the tarred driveway of Pit Plain farm. Bear right to a lane, Point ❸.

Cross to a track, signposted to New Road, to take a stile on the left just before a walled graveyard. At the next corner of the graveyard

bear right over another stile, and go down a path into a wooded hollow ahead. The path bears up the right-hand side of the hollow, to a stile into a field. Bear right, around the slope with a fence just below, passing two sheds to a field gate. Just below is a road, Point ❸.

Follow this lane, Dray Road, to the left to join a larger road, and keep ahead on this to the imposing gateway of New Lodge. Go through the gates on to a gravel track under a fine avenue of oaks. At its end, Montacute House appears ahead in an unexpected back view. This is Point ❹.

Here turn down left past an isolated stile towards Montacute church and St Michael's Tower above. At the far side of the field is a small gate (the field boundary being a fence to the right of this gate and a hedge to its left): this leads into the gardens of Montacute House. Keep ahead, through three stone gateways, then turn left to the lodge and the main street of the village, with the King's Arms up to the right. Continue on Walk 23 picking up at Point ❹.

Winsham and Wayford

A walk between two remarkable villages, featuring two very different churches, hidden in the chalk combes of south-west Somerset.

DISTANCE 7 miles (11.3km)	**MINIMUM TIME** 3hrs 30min
ASCENT/GRADIENT 900t (274m) ▲▲▲	**LEVEL OF DIFFICULTY** +++

PATHS Byways, tracks (some tarred), minor roads, field-edges, 3 stiles
LANDSCAPE Gently rolling hills
SUGGESTED MAP OS Explorer 116 Lyme Regis & Bridport
START / FINISH Grid reference: ST 375063
DOG FRIENDLINESS Dogs can be off lead along byways
PARKING Street parking near Bell Inn
PUBLIC TOILETS None en route

WALK 25 DIRECTIONS

Winsham is a lovely village, with houses in Mediterranean colours of yellow and pink as well as the golden Hamstone. Winsham church is essentially medieval. This is because after 1550 official Protestantism under Edward VI saw much church decoration removed or destroyed. For the rest of that century each new monarch had the old vicar removed for having the 'wrong' religion. Understandably, the wealthy stopped leaving their money to the church and left it to their descendants instead –

the grand buildings of Tudor and Stuart times were not churches but country houses.

At the foot of Winsham's main street turn left into Court Street, and at its end keep ahead, with footpath signs for Wayford. The path becomes a track. Where another track crosses, keep ahead into a field, to pass to the right of Broadenham Farm with its handsome Hamstone porch. Follow waymarkers to the left of farm buildings to a lane. Turn right and follow the lane to Hey Farm. A track with waymarkers leads round to the right of the buildings, and then bends to the right. Follow it through Ashcombe Farm – the track between the buildings is a permitted path. In another 0.5 mile (800m) you reach the parking area at the foot of Wayford Wood.

Go through a gate to a noticeboard with a map. Wayford Wood is more of an exotic shrubbery, with unusual trees, rhododendron, Japanese maple

WHILE YOU'RE THERE

Forde Abbey isn't among Somerset's superb collection of early country houses – it is actually 150yds (137m) into Dorset. A superb medieval abbey, transformed in 1649, it has one of the finest and most varied selections of ceilings in the country. The gardens are also magnificent, with many water features including the former moat.

and bluebells in season. Take the main path, up to right of the noticeboard. At the top of the wood, paths bend right. With the wood edge just above, turn down to the right and descend to steps back onto the track, now 350yds (200m) along from the car park.

Turn left for 0.25 mile (400m) into Wayford. A golden manor house, a few stone cottages and a tiny church make up the village, with a single road leading out to the rest of the world. Keep ahead to the chapel, barely bigger than a room. In this small, undecorated space, you might feel God is sitting right beside you. (You can divert through the churchyard to rejoin the lane beyond.)

At the end of the village, at 'Give Way' markings, turn left up the steep and hedged Chard Lane. At the top of the hill, opposite a side road, turn left through a gate with signpost. A faint track runs across the field, keeping up left of a farm in a dip. At the field end, turn left to a stile, go around an oak tree, and find the corner of a farm track. Follow this ahead, with a hedge on your right (rather than down right to the farm). After 100yds (91m) the track bends left: here climb a gate ahead and follow the hedge on your right to the field corner and a gate into a lane. Turn right for 220yds (201m) then left into a concrete farm track signposted for Chalkway. The track leads through Midnell Farm and then Lue Farm, where it passes through a large shed. After 0.25 mile (400m) it joins a road.

Turn left, down into a gloomy wood of larches, and then right, over a cattle grid, on to a tarred track. This runs through parkland,

to reach a lane. Turn left, down over a mossy bridge, over the crest of a hill, and down towards Winsham. Just above the village a stile on the left is signed for Back Street. Cross a field corner to pass to the left of some houses. Another stile leads into the village: turn downhill to reach the Bell Inn. Don't miss the church.

Winsham church is unusual for having retained its rood screen. This carved partition between the congregation and the altar was particularly objectionable to the Protestant style-police. Even more remarkable is the painted tympanum, the wooden panel that filled the space above the screen. This 14th-century crucifixion scene lay under whitewash throughout the Reformation and it was not rediscovered until Victorian times. We are so accustomed to the Victorian-piety style of religious painting – pale people, eyes turned heavenwards – that this down-to-earth painting comes as a refreshing shock.

Coneygore Hill and Cucklington

WALK 26

Up and down the hill in deepest Somerset, taking in a church with over a thousand years of history.

DISTANCE 5.5 miles (8.8km)	**MINIMUM TIME** 2hrs 45min
ASCENT/GRADIENT 600ft (183m) ▲▲▲	**LEVEL OF DIFFICULTY** +++

PATHS Little-used field paths, which may be overgrown, 11 stiles
LANDSCAPE Small hills grazed by cows
SUGGESTED MAP OS Explorer 129 Yeovil & Sherborne
START / FINISH Grid reference: ST 747298
DOG FRIENDLINESS Route over pasture so on lead or under close control
PARKING Lay-by on former main road immediately south of A303
PUBLIC TOILETS None en route

Throughout the Middle Ages sheep brought increasing prosperity to Somerset. And the merchants, spinners and clothiers could think of no better way to spend their wool money than in glorifying God. With the monasteries becoming ever richer and less religious, the good Somerset yeoman preferred to praise God and improve his village by making a donation to his parish church.

Somerset Churches

So, in every corner of the county, in the Norman style or in the sturdy simplicity of the English Gothic, there rose the church towers of Somerset. By the end of the 12th century there were nearly 500 of them – 21 of our 50 walks involve a church. The towers of yellow limestone rose above thatched villages, cornfields and green fields. They provided waymarkers for wanderers among the ditches and reed beds. The church ale, or fund-raising party, was the main social event of the village. ('Ale' is an archaic word for festival, at which this liquor was drunk.)

Early English and Decorated

The Norman style of church is recognisable by its round arches. Few such churches have survived in England. Many of the later churches, including Cucklington, retain their Norman font. The Early English is the beginning of the Gothic, pointy-arch style. The windows are single and narrow, called 'lancets'. Interior decoration often uses the polished, pale-grey limestone from Dorset known as Purbeck marble. Wells Cathedral, with its ornate front and breathtaking inverted arch is the crowning glory of the Early English style. The Gothic was essentially a new way of building stone structures that didn't fall down. As the builders got more skilful, they were able to leave out more of the stone. From about 1300, the style called Decorated has compound windows, in three or five panels, like the west window at Cucklington.

Somerset has few Perpendicular churches; a rare example is seen in St Barbara's Chapel in Cucklington. St Barbara herself, patron saint of hills was shown locked up in a tower by her heathen papa. In fact Cucklington church was built and rebuilt over several centuries – study it closely and it's a history of the last thousand years. St Barbara's Chapel was a chantry, where prayers were said for some rich benefactor. Around 1500 such short-cuts to heaven were deemed unseemly, and the chapel was incorporated into the body of the church. Unfortunately the people in the chapel couldn't see the priest, so they built the peculiar peephole that's called a hagioscope or squint. The church owes its feeling of space and simplicity to the wrecking activities of the Puritans. There is a colourful and enthusiastic royal coat of arms, painted at the restoration of Charles II. The roof was put back on again after the great storm of 1705.

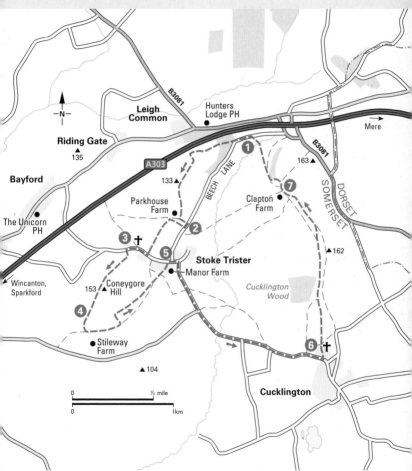

WALK 26 DIRECTIONS

❶ With the A303 on your right, walk on along the lane to where a track runs ahead into a wood. At its far side a fenced footpath runs near the main road. Turn left up a path, then right into a fenced-in path that bends round to the left to reach Parkhouse Farm. After an uncomfortably nettly passage (in summer) to the left of the buildings, turn again left to a lane.

❷ Turn back right, to follow the field-edge back alongside

CUCKLINGTON

the farm track. Go through one field gate and at once turn left through another. Aiming towards Stoke Trister church, follow the left edge of one field and then go straight up a second, turning right along a lane to reach the church.

WHAT TO LOOK OUT FOR

Coneygore, or 'Coneygar', is a rabbit warren. Rabbits were introduced by the Normans as a convenience food; just dig them out a bank to burrow into, and send out two men with a ferret and a net at dinner time.

❸ Continue for 170yds (155m) to a stile and gate on the left. Go up a track, but turn right alongside the hedge above, passing a mobile phone mast on your right. Follow the hedge around the rim of Coneygore Hill, over one stile, to a second with a wide view ahead.

❹ Head straight down towards Stileway Farm. But half-way down, turn left and contour across fields to a stile, and then to a gate

WHILE YOU'RE THERE

With this walk so handy for the A303, it might be appropriate to take in the Haynes Motor Museum at Sparkford. The Model J Duesenberg Tourer is worth a cool $1,000,000, the Sinclair C5 and Prince Harry's go-kart rather less.

with cattle trough and stile above. (Or a track just above the farm leads across into this same field's foot.) Head uphill, with the hedge now on your left, to the steeper bank around Coneygore Hill. Turn right and follow this banking to cross a stile. Keep level through a tree gap, then slant down to the right, below a tiny vineyard, to reach a stile behind. The path ahead contours forward to a lane near Manor Farm.

❺ Turn downhill past a thatched cottage, and bear right for Cucklington. There are field paths on the left, but it's simpler to use this lane to cross the valley and climb to Cucklington village. A gravel track on the left leads to Cucklington church.

❻ Pass to the left of the church, and contour across two fields, passing above Cucklington Wood. In the third field slant up to the right to join a track, which leads to Clapton Farm.

❼ After the Tudor manor house the track bends right, uphill. Turn left between farm buildings to a gate beside a phone mast, and then turn left again down a wooded bank. Turn right, along the base of the bank, to a gap in a grown-out hedge. Now bear left past a power pole to the field's bottom corner. Cross a footbridge under hazels to a second and a stile beyond. Then, go straight up to a stile by a cattle trough and the lane you parked on.

Cadbury Castle as Camelot?

A hill-fort gives wide views of Somerset and a glimpse of pre-history.

DISTANCE **6.5 miles (10.4km)**   MINIMUM TIME **3hrs 30min**

ASCENT/GRADIENT **1,000ft (305m) ▲▲▲**   LEVEL OF DIFFICULTY **+++**

PATHS *Well-used paths, 7 stiles*

LANDSCAPE *Steep-sided, green hills*

SUGGESTED MAP *OS Explorer 129 Yeovil & Sherborne*

START / FINISH *Grid reference: ST 632253*

DOG FRIENDLINESS *Mixed farming: reasonable freedom*

PARKING *Cadbury Castle car park (free), south of South Cadbury*

PUBLIC TOILETS *None en route*

Cadbury Castle was a military stronghold for over 4,000 years. The ditches and earth walls first rose in the Stone Age, and were extended in the Bronze Age. In the Iron Age it became the capital of the Durotinges tribe, who gave their name to Dorset. Here they built a town of wood, willow-wattle and thatch and held out against the Romans. The Romans won in the end: they burnt down the hilltop town in around AD 70.

The Saxon, Ethelred the Unready, repaired the fort against the Vikings. Again it became a wartime capital, replacing Ilchester between 1009 and 1019. Coins were minted here, and labelled 'CADANBYRIC'.

The local belief that Cadbury is indeed King Arthur's Camelot was first recorded in 1542 – more than 1,000 years after King Arthur. However, it was supported by excavations in the 1960s, which showed that, at the very time of the legendary King Arthur, the walls were rebuilt in timber and stone. Some of this stonework is visible on the left as you return to the track down off the hill. A large and kingly timber hall rose on the hilltop. Finds of pottery imported from the eastern Mediterranean indicate a place of wealth and good taste.

In this wooden hall the various strands of legend converge. We can imagine rich tapestries hanging from the panelled walls, and below them the court intrigues and amours, described by the 15th-century Sir Thomas Malory. It's even easier to see Queen Guenevere and her ladies riding out along Corton Ridge to gather may-blossom. But at the end of a short mid-winter's day, in the darkness under the trees, the pre-Christian, holly-bearing Green Knight of the anonymous Gawain Poet comes striding up the long earthen ramp. And if he did exist, it was very possibly from here that Arthur and his knights went forth to the battle of Mons Badonis, which may have been at Bath, to conquer the Saxon; and later to defeat at the bloody battle of Camlann.

Like most of the limestone hillocks of Somerset that made such fine forts, Cadbury has a wide view over the Levels. The viewpoint cairn was raised at the Millennium; in accordance with the Arthurian environment, the places indicated are mostly mystic and invisible. The eye of faith and

SOUTH CADBURY

legend sees behind the horizon to Stonehenge, Avebury and Tintagel. But in winter, the actual eye can trace the possible route of Arthur's final journey, through the flooded fields of the Somerset Levels. Legend would have it that three queens in a black barge carried him through the high water to Glastonbury, on Avalon Isle, knowing his wound was a deadly one. And there he supposedly rests, hidden in the hill, waiting to be called to defend Britain in her hour of need.

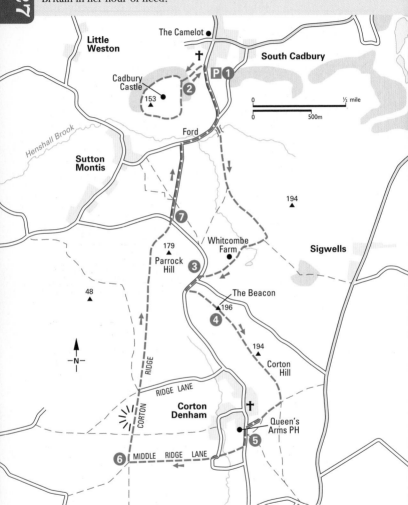

WALK 27 DIRECTIONS

1 Turn right out of the car park to the first house in South Cadbury. A stony track leads up on to Cadbury Castle. The earth ramparts and top of the fort are Access Land, so you can stroll around at will.

2 Return past the car park. After 0.25 mile (400m) you pass a side road on the left, to reach a stile marked 'Sigwells'. Go straight down to a stile and footbridge. Follow the left edge of a field then an uncultivated strip. A track runs ahead, but take a stile on the right to follow the field-edge next to

SOUTH CADBURY

it, then a line of hawthorns ahead, to a gate with two waymarkers. A faint track leads along the top of the following field. At its end turn down into a hedged earth track. This leads out past Whitcombe Farm to rejoin the road.

3 Turn left to a junction below Corton Denham Beacon. Keep right for 80yds (73m) to a stile up left. Backtrack above the hedge to the very steep spur of Corton Hill, and go up it (or more gently slant up left above trees), to the summit trig point.

4 Head along the steep hill rim with steep drops to Corton Denham on the right and soon with a fence on the left. You pass a modern 'tumulus', a small, covered reservoir. Above five large lime trees slant gently down to a small, waymarked gate. A green path slants down again, until a gate lets you on to a tarred lane; follow this until you reach the road below.

5 Turn left on the road, which is narrow between high banks, for 170yds (155m) to a stile on the right, 'Middle Ridge Lane'. Go straight across, left of a tree and ditch line, to a hidden stile into a lane. Keep ahead on a stony track that climbs gently to the ridgeline.

6 Turn right, and walk along Corton Ridge with a hedge on the right and a wide view on the left. After 650yds (594m) Ridge Lane starts on the right, but go through a small gate on the left to continue along the ridge. After a final gate a

green path bends around the flank of Parrock Hill. With Cadbury Castle now on the left, the main path turns left to a hedge corner and waymarked gate. A hedged path leads to a road.

7 Cross into a road signed 'South Cadbury'. After 700yds (640m) turn right, again for South Cadbury, and follow the road round the base of Cadbury Castle to the car park.

Edge of the Levels

From Polden's edge down on to the Somerset Levels and up again.

DISTANCE *4.5 miles (7.2km)*   MINIMUM TIME *2hrs 15min*

ASCENT/GRADIENT *450ft (137m)* ▲▲▲   LEVEL OF DIFFICULTY +++

PATHS *Initially steep then easy tracks and paths, 3 stiles*

LANDSCAPE *Water-meadows of the Somerset Levels, and wooded heights above*

SUGGESTED MAP *OS Explorer 141 Cheddar Gorge*

START / FINISH *Grid reference: ST 480345*

DOG FRIENDLINESS *Off lead on drove tracks and in woods*

PARKING *Car park (free) at Street Youth Hostel, just off B3151; another car park on south side of road*

PUBLIC TOILETS *None en route; nearest are at Street*

O f Somerset's six hill ranges, the Poldens are the smallest; they rise to just 400ft (122m) at Great Breach Wood. Along the hedged A39 the car driver won't have any feeling of being on a summit ridge. The passengers, however, will be getting glimpses, between the branches, of wide lands on either side. And if you get out and stand at the top of the southern scarp, the long, windswept edge above the Levels is almost like the top of a sea cliff. In fact, a sea cliff is what it once was. The Bristol Channel has flowed over the Levels several times in the last few millennia – and still does, occasionally, during winter floods. To the north, the village of Burtle stands not on peat but on a sandbank with seashells. Glastonbury Tor and Brent Knoll were formed as islands undercut by the waves.

Hardy's Tragic Poem

This high, dry ridge has been a road since Roman times. An inn stood at Marshall's Elm, now the site of the Street Youth Hostel and the start of our walk. An incident here provoked Thomas Hardy (1840–1928) to put pen to paper. *A Trampwoman's Tragedy* (1902) concerns flirtation and murder, and was turned down by the editor of Cornhill magazine in the United States as 'not a poem he could possibly print in a family periodical'. Despite being set in Somerset, Hardy considered it his most successful poem – and much shorter than any of the Dorset novels.

> 'And as the sun drew down to west,
> We climb the toilsome Polden crest,
> And saw, of landskip sights the best,
> The inn that beamed thereby.
> Beneath us figured tor and lea,
> From Mendip to the western sea –
> I doubt if finer sight there be
> Within this royal realm.'

POLDEN HILLS

Given the Polden status as a former sea cliff, it's quite appropriate that one of England's admirals should stand on Windmill Hill, in the shape of a stone column. Samuel Hood, born 1724, is perhaps England's seventh most famous admiral. He entered the navy as a teenager, and rose to distinguish himself as a bad-tempered but effective commander. American historians seem relieved that, during the Battle of the Capes in Chesapeake Bay in 1781, a bad decision by Admiral Rodney left Hood a bystander while the Royal Navy suffered one of its worst-ever defeats.

In the early part of the Napoleonic War, Hood served in the Mediterranean. He mounted a successful raid on Toulon in 1793; a junior officer on the raiding party, one Horatio Nelson, was wounded by flying gravel thrown up by a cannonball and lost the sight in one eye. Hood retired the next year, and died in 1814 after seeing his tactical ideas triumphantly continued by young Nelson.

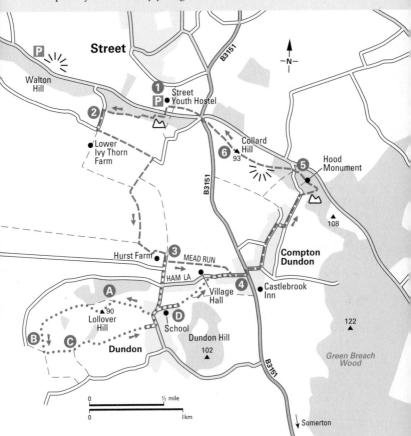

WALK 28 DIRECTIONS

❶ From the parking area on the youth hostel side, cross and turn right on a woodland path. After 100yds (91m) a smaller path descends on the left by some steps. At the foot of the wood turn right, and at a field corner go down a little to reach another track. This runs along the base of the wood to a lane.

② Go down to the entrance of Lower Ivy Thorn Farm, and turn left into a track. After 0.5 mile (800m) this reaches the corner of an unsurfaced road, where you turn right. After 0.25 mile (400m) the track turns left into a field. Follow its edge, with a ditch and fence to your left, to a gate at the field corner. In the next field continue alongside the ditch to the corner. The former footbridge is derelict under brambles. Take a gate on the left, then turn right. The field-edge zig-zags to pass to the left of Hurst Farm, leading to a tarred lane.

WHERE TO EAT AND DRINK

The Castlebrook Inn in Compton Dundon is a short distance from Point ❹. This old coaching inn welcomes dogs and children, and serves bar meals and real scrumpy cider.

③ Turn right to reach a bridleway sign on the left. Follow this green track until it joins Ham Lane. Follow this lane to reach the crossroads of the B3151 in Compton Dundon, with the Castlebrook Inn to your right.

④ Cross the busy B3151 and pass between an ancient market cross (right) and a granite Victorian obelisk (left) into Compton Street. At the first junction keep round to the left, towards the Hood Monument above. As the street starts to climb, turn right and left up the lane beyond – signposted 'Butleigh'. Where it reaches woodland bear right, up a steep fenced path, ignoring stiles on the left. The path slants up into the wood. Then, some 35yds (32m) before it arrives at a road, turn left along the top of the steep ground, to the Hood Monument.

WHILE YOU'RE THERE

From the Middle Ages onwards, the affluence and development of the Somerset Levels was signalled by the number of windmills along the Polden ridge. Stembridge Tower Mill at High Ham is more recent, dating from 1822. It has been restored by the National Trust, though not yet into full working order.

⑤ Continue down through the wood to a minor road, with the main road 50yds (46m) away on the right. Ignore a path descending opposite but turn right for a few steps to a footpath sign and a kissing gate. A grass path heads gently up the crest of Collard Hill, with wide views to the left.

⑥ From the summit go straight on down to a stile and the signposted crossroads of the B3151. Cross both roads. The ridge road is signposted for the youth hostel, and your path is just to its right. It crosses a glade into woodland. Keep to the right of some hummocky ground to the wood's edge, and follow this path to the car park.

WHAT TO LOOK OUT FOR

The medieval market cross passed in Compton Dundon is constructed of yellow Hamstone, its edges softened by the weathering of the centuries. The obelisk is of imported granite, polished to a hard shine that will never weather.

Loll Over Lollover Hill

*A Polden outlier, ideal for picnics and for viewing
the surrounding ranges.*

See map and information panel for Walk 28

DISTANCE *7 miles (11.3km)*   MINIMUM TIME *3hrs 30min*
ASCENT/GRADIENT *850ft (259m)* ▲▲▲   LEVEL OF DIFFICULTY ✦✦✦
DOG FRIENDLINESS *English Nature asks that dogs be on leads within SSSI*

WALK 29 DIRECTIONS
(Walk 28 option)

This simple round of Lollover
Hill can be done as an extension
to Walk 28, or as a self-contained
short walk (3 miles/4.8km),
starting from Compton Dundon
village hall on Ham Lane.

From Hurst Farm (Point ❸
on Walk 28) carry straight on
down the access road to cross
Ham Lane into Dundon village.
The street bends right below
the church and then sharply left.
At this corner earth steps lead
up on the right, with a waymarker
for Lollover Hill. Pass between
hedges to an earth track, and turn
right. The track bends left and
then heads uphill. A stile leads
into the Site of Special Scientific
Interest (SSSI) around Lollover
summit, Point Ⓐ.

Fork up left to the trig point,
then rejoin the track at the stile
and gate where it leaves the other
end of the SSSI. After another
stile follow the hedge ahead,
walking on its left. Ignore a stile
and footbridge on the right, and
continue down the spur to yet
another stile. The hedge now
bends left to a gate, Point Ⓑ.

Cross the top edge of the field
beyond, to its corner, with a gate

on the left (ignore waymarked
stile ahead here). Go through
this gate and walk along the next
field, 30yds (27m) out from its
right-hand hedge, to a stile over
an electric fence leading to a track
corner, Point Ⓒ. Walk up the
track ahead through a wood, then
between hedges. It descends to
become a lane into Dundon.

Turn left up the village street, go
round the sharp right-hand bend
and fork right past the school
(Point Ⓓ). Where the lane ends,
a track runs ahead. After 60yds
(55m) take a gate on the left, and
follow the church path – a half-
buried line of flagstones. Take a
gate on the left and turn right, still
on flagstones, to cross the corner
of a field into a small wood. The
path passes between steadings,
through three more gates. Cross a
final field diagonally left to a gate
leading out on to Ham Lane near
the village hall.

To continue on Walk 28 turn
right, noting in the verge the
continuing flagstones of the
church path. The lane reaches the
B3151 at Point ❹.

WALK 30

Medieval Marketing and Geology at Glastonbury

Legend, geology and architecture combined: King Arthur, a sacred thorn, a Somerset tor and ten centuries of fine buildings.

DISTANCE 2.5 miles (4km)   MINIMUM TIME 1hr 30min

ASCENT/GRADIENT 500ft (152m) ▲▲▲   LEVEL OF DIFFICULTY +++

PATHS Streets, well-built paths on tor; muddy path on Chalice Hill

LANDSCAPE Busy tourist town and small, steep hill

SUGGESTED MAP OS Explorer 141 Cheddar Gorge

START / FINISH Grid reference: ST 498389

DOG FRIENDLINESS Urban walk, with lead requested on tor

PARKING St John's pay-and-display, Northload Street

PUBLIC TOILETS St John's car park and at abbey entrance

WALK 30 DIRECTIONS

From the Market Cross head down Magdalene Street, past the entrance to the Glastonbury Abbey grounds. On the right is the 18th-century Pump Room, indicating Glastonbury's brief period as a spa town. Just beyond it is St Margaret's Chapel, originally a 14th-century hospice for pilgrims.

We must leave aside the stories of King Arthur and Joseph of Arimathaea, enjoyable as they are, for we now know they were invented to raise visitor revenue for rebuilding works after the fire of 1184. This was a strategy which must surely qualify as the most persistent and effective advertising campaign of all time. Money was raised by the sale of indulgences (time-off-purgatory vouchers) and relics, and still flows into shops and offertory boxes today.

Cross a roundabout (with, on the right, the road to Street logically named 'Street Road' – it couldn't really have been 'Street Street'),

keep ahead into Fishers Hill, then follow the main road left into Bere Lane. Follow this to its end, passing the Rural Life Museum in Abbey Barn – once a grange barn of Glastonbury Abbey.

At Chilkwell Street turn right on to a raised pavement. After 0.25 mile (400m) you reach the Chalice Well and Gardens: its sinister blood-red waters once supplied the abbey, and later the Pump House. It has been developed as a 'visitor attraction' (with an entry fee). Turn left into Well House

WHILE YOU'RE THERE

Visit Glastonbury Abbey. Among these hallowed ruins it's hard not to believe the legend that Joseph of Arimathaea brought the child Jesus to England, and built here a simple church of woven willow branches. Even without Arthur of Avalon, we still have an important abbey site with genuine Celtic roots; a showcase of the best of late medieval and Tudor architecture, and a hill with some of the best views in the county.

Right: Glastonbury Abbey (Walk 30)

Lane and at once right, up a steep lane that leads on to Glastonbury Tor. The hill is made of layers of clay and blue limestone, with a cap of sandstone. Once the resistant sandstone has eroded away the tor will quickly collapse – but a geological age or two must pass before this happens. A dense cloud of legend and mystery hangs over Glastonbury Tor. This was a sacred site for the pagans, and then for over 1,000 years the Christian heart of the West Country.

A concrete path with steps leads upwards. Kestrels hover in the updraft of the steep sides. At the top is St Michael's Tower, left over from a medieval chapel: this has been a sacred site since the 6th century, with an earlier chapel having collapsed in an earthquake. Richard Whiting, the last Abbot of Glastonbury, was hanged, drawn and quartered here for resisting the Dissolution of the monasteries under Henry VIII. His dismembered parts were then displayed in nearby towns.

Turn right, in the direction of a reservoir far below, to find a concrete path that spirals down to the left. At the hill foot it turns right to a kissing gate. Cross Moneybox Field to a gate on to a lane. Turn left along the lane, with Glastonbury Tor up on your left, and bear left at a junction. After 140yds (128m) a gate on the right leads into a field. Bear left to another gate. The hedged path beyond gets muddy in winter. Keep ahead down a tarred lane and, where this bends left, take the path ahead. It passes down Chalice Hill with a hedge on its left, to a lane below. At the foot of the lane the arched entrance of Abbey House is ahead. Turn right in Lambrook Street. On a wall on the left is a handsome Victorian

WHAT TO LOOK OUT FOR

Medieval timber-frame cottages get resurfaced again and again through the centuries. Signs to look for are: steep roofs that were formerly thatch; low doorways; small windows; and very thick walls (shown at the window-openings). Examples at the walk start are Nos 1 and 2 Market Place.

fire-plate, indicating the nearby water supply, and at the junction of High Street is an old fountain.

Turn left to pass all the way along High Street. Almost every building here is noteworthy. St John's churchyard has a Glastonbury thorn – a cutting from the original miraculous thorn that grew from the staff of Joseph of Arimathaea. The thorn is supposed to flower twice, at Christmas and Easter.

On the left, a Victorian shopfront stands beside the arch of the former White Horse Inn: here some of the losers were hanged after the Monmouth Rebellion of 1685. The information centre is housed behind a Tudor façade of around 1500. At the end of High Street is the Market Cross, with the King William pub standing invitingly behind it.

WHERE TO EAT AND DRINK

There is a wide selection of cafés and inns around Market Place, the most striking being the George and Pilgrim hotel, which was built in the 14th century to accommodate overflow from the abbey's own hostelry.

More Borders at Three County Corner

An expedition through parts of Somerset, Dorset and Wiltshire, to Stourhead and Alfred's Tower.

DISTANCE	8.5 miles (13.7km) MINIMUM TIME 4hrs
ASCENT/GRADIENT	750ft (229m) ▲▲▲ LEVEL OF DIFFICULTY ✦✦✦
PATHS	Some tracks and some small paths and field-edges, 17 stiles
LANDSCAPE	Tree-covered ridge
SUGGESTED MAP	OS Explorer 142 Shepton Mallet
START / FINISH	Grid reference: ST 755314
DOG FRIENDLINESS	Moderate freedom on tracks and in woodland
PARKING	Pen Selwood church; some verge parking at Bleak Farm
PUBLIC TOILETS	Near Spread Eagle Inn – from Point ⑤ continue through arch for 0.25 mile (400m)

Patriotic English people tend to think of Arthur and of Alfred, almost interchangeably, as the first king of their land; this is odd, as they were mortal enemies. Arthur, if he existed, ruled the Britons: a small, dark, Celtic people who spoke what we now call Old Welsh. Alfred spoke Old English, and belonged to the Saxon invaders. Eventually the invaders were themselves attacked by the Vikings and so started to think of themselves as the home side. Arthur's kingdom was Logres – which may or may not have been somewhere hereabouts.

Alfred, King of Somerset

Alfred was King of Somerset and, beyond that, King of Wessex; England had yet to be invented. Somerset, however, was a civilisation worth fighting for. Alfred fortified Burrow Mump (see Walk 36) as a strongpoint against the Danes, whose longships came at him up the River Parrett.

Defeated, he took refuge in the swamps of the 'Sumer Saete'. It was on the marsh island of Muchelney, south of Langport, that the demoralised and preoccupied King took shelter in the winter of AD 878 in a swine-herd's mud hut. The peasant's wife set him to watch the cakes, with disastrous results for the cookery but an eventual good outcome for Wessex... Emerging from his fen island, Alfred gathered the Saxons at Egbert's Stone, probably at the present-day site of Alfred's Tower. He defeated the Danes at Edington, now in Wiltshire.

A Wise King

Alfred reigned from AD 873 to 888. He set up burhs, fortified towns, at Axbridge, Bath (where he reused the Roman defences), Langport and Watchet. His palace was at Cheddar. Alfred was a wise king who mixed thoughtfulness with ruthlessness, and realised that government based partly on consent was easier and worked better than government by force. His laws were put to a (non-elected) parliament of his witan: churchmen, nobles and local leaders.

ALFRED'S TOWER

The tower on this walk was placed in romantic commemoration of King Alfred; but its real point is as a place to turn round at the top of a scenic carriage drive from Stourhead – the turning circle for the carriages is still visible in the grass.

Modern Follies

Today, while we decorate the hills with various money-making structures such as phone masts and television transmitters, to build a tower simply for decorative effect would as likely as not be dismissed instantly as a wicked intrusion on the landscape. There is a small charge if you want to go up the tower, but if its a clear day, it's the only way to get above the treetops for the total, three-county view.

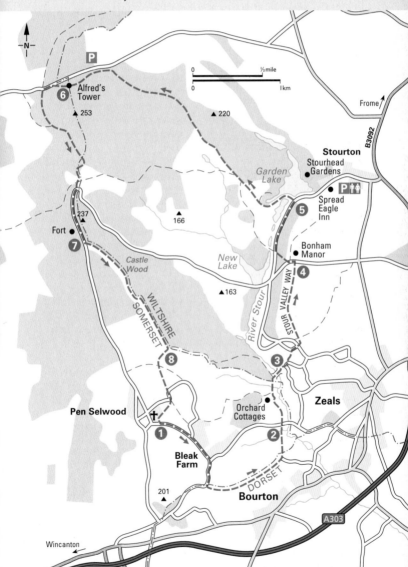

WALK 31 DIRECTIONS

1 Go to the right through the churchyard to join a road beyond. Turn left through Bleak Farm village, bear right 'Bourton', then left into an inconspicuous sunken track. This ends at the top of a tarred lane; here turn left through a white gate, signed 'Pen Mill Hill'. The path on the right heads diagonally down a field to to a kissing gate in a dip. Follow a green track past a pond to a road.

WHILE YOU'RE THERE

Visit the National Trust's Stourhead House. The lakes and ornamental buildings are glimpsed on the walk: for a fuller view of the ornamental water and temples you'll have to pay,

---

2 From here to Point **4** is marked 'Stour Valley Way'. Cross on to a path waymarked 'Coombe Street'. Pass below Orchard Cottages, then turn up left over a stile, and right over another. Cross a stream in a dip to a stile below a thatched cottage. A woodland path bends to the right to a footbridge over the tiny River Stour.

3 Go up on a tarred lane and turn left briefly. Keep ahead into a hedged way for 30yds (27m) to a stile on the right. Go up and round left to another stile. The lane beyond leads to a T-junction; go across and turn left on to a bridleway track. Go through a gate to follow the left edge of a field into a hedged track to emerge opposite Bonham Manor.

4 Turn left, and at the second signpost bear right to a road below. Follow this to the right, to a rustic rock arch. A track on the left is signposted 'Alfred's Tower'.

5 The main track (blue arrows) heads into a wooded valley with Alfred's Tower visible ahead. At a fork take the track ahead, along the foot of the wood then into it. Finally it reaches open ground at the hilltop, with a road ahead. Turn left, in a grassy avenue, to Alfred's Tower.

6 Join the road ahead for 220yds (201m), down to a sunken path on the left signed 'Penselwood'. Follow this, ignoring paths on both sides, on to a track descending to a major junction. Here bear right to a lane. Bear right again, on a tarmac road signed 'Penselwood'. This leads over a hilltop containing a Roman fort. At the road's highest point, open ground appears on the left.

7 Cross a stile to go forward 40yds (37m) then bend to the right down a grassy glade. This gives way to field-edges with stiles, the mature trees of Castle Wood still on your left. After several fields, a gate on the left would lead into the wood.

8 Don't go through the gate, instead turn right around the foot of the field to two gates on the left, keep right over two stiles then bear left down two fields to a road bend. Keep ahead to a sharp right-hand bend, where the right-hand of two gates starts a field path to Pen Selwood church.

WHERE TO EAT AND DRINK

The Spread Eagle Inn (no dogs) is at the entrance to Stourhead House. To get there from Point **5** keep ahead through the rock arch for 0.25 mile (400m).

Bruton Combes

A walk around and above beautiful Bruton,
a typical Somerset town, built in the early wealth
of the wool industry.

WALK 32

DISTANCE *4.5 miles (7.2km)*	MINIMUM TIME *2hrs 15min*

ASCENT/GRADIENT *350ft (107m)* ▲▲▲   LEVEL OF DIFFICULTY +++

PATHS *Enclosed tracks, open fields; no stiles*

LANDSCAPE *Steep, grassy hills and combes*

SUGGESTED MAP *OS Explorer 142 Shepton Mallet*

START / FINISH *Grid reference: ST 684348*

DOG FRIENDLINESS *On lead or under close control*

PARKING *Free parking off Silver Street, 50yds (46m) west of church; larger car park in Upper Backway*

PUBLIC TOILETS *Near Church Bridge (walk start) and signposted from there*

Bruton is a typical Somerset town: originally Saxon but made prosperous by monks in the Middle Ages. The Augustinians moved in around 1150 and soon upgraded from priory to abbey. In the 10th century Bruton was the county's seventh largest town – though this was achieved with a tax-paying population of just 85!

Woolly Thinking

In the Middle Ages England was a one-product economy. The basic unit of wealth was the 346lb (157kg) woolsack. In 1310 some 35,000 of these were exported; in 1421, 75 per cent of all customs duties were paid on wool. In Parliament at London, the Lord Chancellor sat on a woolsack as a constant reminder of where his government's money came from. (Today it has been replaced by a wool-stuffed chair.)

As the price of raw wool started to fall, England turned to the manufacture of cloth, adding value to the product before it left the country. Bruton was ahead of the game here. Back in 1240 the town built its first fulling mill, sited on Quaperlake Street. Here the cloth was washed with fullers' earth, a form of clay that acts as a natural de-greasing compound. (Fuller's earth absorbs water as well as grease; it is responsible for the peculiarly sticky mud encountered on the climb out of Combe Hay on Walk 48.) The washed wool was then felted with water-powered hammers.

The raw wool market had been dominated by trading barons, who frequently became real aristocratic barons as a result. But the cloth trade saw, and to a great extent caused, the rise of the English middle class of clothiers and merchants. Their wool wealth rebuilt the church and a century later added its unusual second tower; they built the High Street and endowed the almshouses. Bruton clothiers traded with merchants in Hampshire, Dorset and London, and exported through the ports of Dorset. In the 1540s Bruton's fullers were importing woad (for dyeing) from the far Azores by way of Bristol. The Abbey saw its interests as parallel with those of the town, and subsidised the market cross and the licensing of fairs.

Wool Unspun

Mechanisation of the spinning and weaving processes was getting under way in the 1820s, but depression set in the 1830s and Somerset never caught up with Lancashire. Hence Somerset wool villages remain non-industrial and pretty. Many medieval buildings survive behind the (fairly) modern shop signs and under the paintwork. Where others have collapsed through the ages, replacements have been inserted in the style of every century but always with sympathy. Today, competition from synthetic materials means the price of a fleece barely pays the wages of the shearer. In Bruton you'll see the evidence of wool wealth on every side, but few sheep.

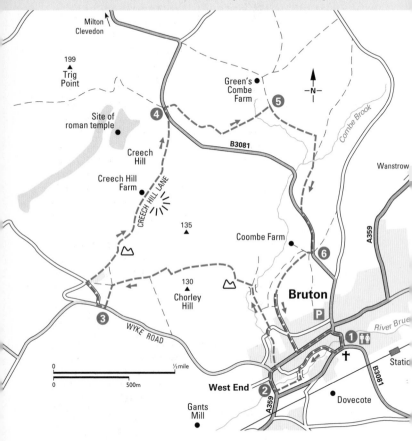

WALK 32 DIRECTIONS

❶ With the church on your left and the bridge on your right, head down Silver Street for 30yds (27m) to a small car park in Coombe Street. The old packhorse bridge over the River Brue leads into Lower Backway. Turn left for 350yds (320m), then take a path between railed fences

to a footbridge. Turn right along the river to A359.

❷ Turn right over Leggs Bridge and right again into the end of High Street, but at once turn off uphill on to a walled path called Mill Dam. At the lane above turn briefly right, then left along byway track signed to Creech Hill Lane. Just after a footbridge fork left:

BRUTON

the hedged path is fairly steep and muddy. At the top of the combe it becomes a farm track. This bends left (the short-cut track on the right isn't a right of way) and reaches Wyke Road.

❸ Turn right for a few steps, then right again, and after 220yds (201m) turn right past farm buildings to an uphill track, Creech Hill Lane. This becomes a hedged tunnel, then emerges at Creech Hill Farm. Once past the cupressus hedge that hides the slurry pit, you'll have a fine view over Bruton. Pass along the front of the farm and out to the B3081.

❹ Head up the road to the first field gate opposite, with bridleway signpost. Turn sharp right to pass below a hedge. The small path follows the rim of the combe hollow. Opposite Green's Combe Farm, slant down left to just below a stream junction – strips of trees mark the streams. Cross the stream and bear left to a gate on to the farm's driveway track.

❺ Turn right, away from the farm, for 220yds (200m) until the track bends right. Here keep ahead through a field gate with a blue waymarker, on to a green track. After 200yds (183m), at the foot of a former hedge, turn downhill, to the left of a row of hazels, to a gate. Pass through a small wood to a gate and track. When this emerges into open field follow the fence above to join the B3081. Turn left, uphill, to the entrance to Coombe Farm.

❻ Ignoring a stile on the left, go down the driveway for barely a dozen paces before turning and at once forking left again on to a wide path under sycamore trees. The path rises gently, with a bank on its left. On reaching a clearing, keep to the left edge to find a descending path that becomes St Catherine's Hill. Weavers' cottages are on the right as the street descends steeply into Bruton. Turn left along the High Street. At its end turn right down Patwell Street to Church Bridge.

Nunney and its Village, Castle and Combe

Visiting a stone-built village with a moated castle, once besieged in the Civil War, on this wander through woodland and pasture.

DISTANCE 3 miles (4.8km) **MINIMUM TIME** 1hr 15min	
ASCENT/GRADIENT 160ft (49m) ▲▲▲ **LEVEL OF DIFFICULTY** +++	
PATHS Broad, riverside path, pasture, then leafy track, no stiles	
LANDSCAPE Deeply wooded stream valley, breaking out into open pasture with wide open views	
SUGGESTED MAP OS Explorer 142 Shepton Mallet	
START / FINISH Grid reference: ST 736456	
DOG FRIENDLINESS Well-behaved dogs can run free in Nunney Combe and on final track	
PARKING Short-stay parking at Nunney Market Square; small lay-by at end of a public footpath 150yds (137m) up Castle Hill	
PUBLIC TOILETS None en route	

The castle at Nunney is awkward to spot, huddled down among the houses, but once found it will not be forgotten. Built in 1373 by Sir John de la Mare, it's a superb structure with large corner towers and a proper moat all the way round. Sir John had fought with the Black Prince in France, and his gatehouse here included some of the very latest French fashions in construction. Through its ruined walls we catch glimpses of the swans and ducks in the moat and the rose-hung cottages of the village.

Costume Drama

The nearby village church, which is attractive in its own right, has interesting effigies of the De la Mere family over two centuries. Such effigies are of particular interest to costume designers, who otherwise would have no idea of what Elizabethan outfits looked like from the back. This is important when you're making a film such as *Shakespeare in Love* — Gwyneth Paltrow can't always be facing the camera! Also worth a look is the font cover from 1684, which is an ornate cone of carved wood.

Uncivil War

Although particular towns had particular loyalties during the Civil War (Wells for Royalist, Taunton for Parliamentarian), Somerset as a whole was not carried away into warfare. Indeed, a local, low-technology force of 'Clubmen' (the first bouncers?) was formed to discourage either side from entering the county. Armies brought inconvenience: 'such uncivil drinkers and thirsty souls that a barrel of good beer trembles at the sight of them, and the whole house nothing but a rendezvous of tobacco and spitting' wrote a Tolland farmer obliged to play host to the Parliamentarians in 1647. Still, Britain's civil wars must be considered civilised when compared with the Thirty Years' War which ravaged Germany around the same time, where the resulting famine and plague reduced the population of the countryside by a third of its former size.

NUNNEY

Taunton was besieged twice, and Bridgwater once. Somerset saw one battle, at Langport. Part of the Royalist army under Lord Goring had arrived too late to get defeated at the Battle of Naseby: Fairfax and the New Model Army caught up with them at the fords of the Wagg Rhyne and defeated them there instead. After the battle, Colonel Prater, its owner, took refuge in Nunney Castle with eight Irishmen. The villagers must have been alarmed at the prospect of a siege taking place right among their houses. In the event the castle fell without much of a fight, although one cannonball lodged in the wall of the nearby church. Afterwards the Roundheads deliberately ruined the castle to prevent its being reoccupied. Somerset's sufferings were to come 40 years later, in the Monmouth Rebellion.

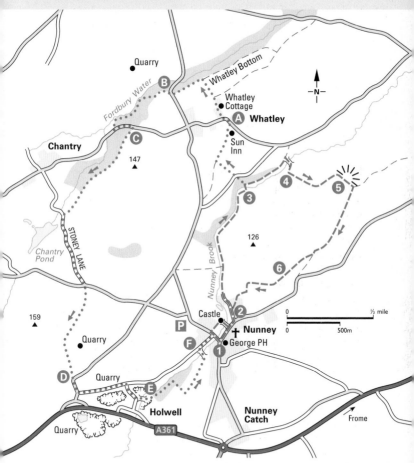

WALK 33 DIRECTIONS

1 From Nunney's Market Place cross the brook and at once turn right to Nunney Castle (entry is free). Having inspected the castle, cross a footbridge towards the church. Turn left in Church Street,

past a stone cross. In another 55yds (50m), where the street starts uphill, bear turn left into Donkey Lane.

2 Follow the lane past a high wall on the left, to a gate with a signpost. Keep ahead, leaving the

99

track after 150yds (137m) for a small gate ahead into woods. A wide path leads downstream with the Nunney Brook on its left. After about 0.75 mile (1.2km) a track runs across the valley.

❸ Turn left, as a signpost suggests, to cross the brook; immediately turn right past a broken stile. Continue along the stream on an often muddy path. After 350yds (320m) the path climbs away from the stream to join a track above. Turn right on this, to cross the stream on a high, arched bridge. The track bends right, through a gate: as it bends back round to the left keep ahead to a waymarked kissing gate on the left.

WHERE TO EAT AND DRINK

The fairly smart George at Nunney has a restaurant and a riverside beer garden (and also a poltergeist). It welcomes children but not dogs. Today it's a peaceful and friendly place, but the garden is believed to have been used for judicial executions and a ghostly woman has been heard wailing.

❹ Go up the right-hand side of a narrow field to a kissing gate. Continue uphill on the left-hand edge for just 65yds (60m) to a kissing gate in the hedge. Turn up right, next to the hedge, then left along the top of the field to a gap at its corner. As this is the crest of a broad ridge, there are now views ahead to the hills in the east.

❺ Head down the left-hand side of the field into a slight dip. Ignore a half-hidden stile on the left but go through the gateway ahead. Now turn half-right and go straight across the field to a visible kissing gate in the skyline hedge – this turns out to be two gates, one

WHILE YOU'RE THERE

On this walk, you could spot a badger's earth (hole) and various birds. For more spectacular wildlife, including the famous lions, head to Longleat, Britain's first safari park. It's just across the Wiltshire border, east of Frome. It's a fairly expensive attraction, so the thrifty will persuade the kids that the fire engine at Frome's (free) museum is just as exciting as Longleat's tigers and rhinos.

behind the other. Once through these, follow the left-hand edge of the long field ahead. At its corner take a kissing gate between two gateways and turn right. The same direction as before, but now with hedge on your right. At the field end cross a farm track via two gates. In another 150yds (137m), a kissing gate is on your right.

WHAT TO LOOK OUT FOR

Less than a century after the Civil War, Nunney had shrugged off its thrilling military history to become a prosperous village of clothiers and weavers. Look out for weavers' cottages with large windows to light the looms. Opposite the church is a riverside ramp: in the 18th century woollen cloth was washed and stretched here.

❻ This leads into a narrow track between over-arching hedges. It bends to the left and then the right, then descends to become a street leading into Nunney. This runs down to join Donkey Lane on the outward route, with the church just 300yds (274m) ahead.

Right: Nunney Castle (Walk 33)

WALK 34

Two Bottoms from Nunney

A longer, more strenuous and slightly brambly ramble.

See map and information panel for Walk 33

> **DISTANCE** 5.25 miles (8.4km) **MINIMUM TIME** 2hrs 45min
> **ASCENT/GRADIENT** 400ft (122m) ▲▲▲ **LEVEL OF DIFFICULTY** ✦✦✦

WALK 34 DIRECTIONS (Walk 33 option)

From Point ❸ cross Nunney Brook and head up to a road. Cross the road to a stile and go up to a kissing gate on the right. Slant diagonally up a big field, to the Sun Inn, Point Ⓐ. Turn left at the next bend, and then turn off right along the driveway to Whatley Cottage. Keep to its left to a gap, and then to the right of a house called Fortywinks. Head straight down, over a stile in new fencing, to the top of the steep wood of Whatley Bottom. Turn left along the field foot to the corner and down to a road, Point Ⓑ.

The path continues opposite, along the top of steep wood. Beyond, a large quarry is removing the landscape. After 200yds (183m) the path slants down past five ancient yew trees to Fordbury Water.

Follow this upstream through woods to a field. Don't enter it, but slant up left to a road. Turn uphill for 220yds (201m) to a footpath on the right, Point Ⓒ. An earth path follows the top edge of the wood (the good path at the foot of the wood is not a right of way). The path descends, to reach Stoney Lane.

Turn left for 0.5 mile (800m) to a road junction. Across slightly left is a green lane between high banks. This passes beside another quarry to reach a busy road, Point Ⓓ. Turn right for 150yds (137m) to a junction. Follow a minor road on the left ('Nunney 1') above yet another quarry, which whitens the hedges with dust. At its end a lane leads steeply downhill. A footpath sign points down to the stream, with a footbridge a few steps away on the left. Turn left, downstream, to pass through an oolitic breeze block depot into a final streamside wood, Point Ⓔ.

After 220yds (201m) the path passes below a small crag and turns uphill to a stile. Continue ahead, at first with the wood on the left, then across open field to a cattle trough. Turn left towards the tower of Nunney church, rejoining the wood edge on the left. Continue along the field-edge above the woodland.

At a wall corner some steps lead down to a footbridge, Point Ⓕ. A walled path leads between gardens into Nunney. Turn right, passing a prison for very small miscreants, to the village centre.

Along the Fosse Way to Shepton Mallet

Catch a bus for this linear stroll along a Roman motorway.

DISTANCE *3.5 miles (5.7km)* **MINIMUM TIME** *1hr 40min*

ASCENT/GRADIENT *300ft (91m)* ▲▲▲ **LEVEL OF DIFFICULTY** ✦✦✦

PATHS *Firm, reasonably mud-free track, field paths, 3 stiles*

LANDSCAPE *Gentle hills of eastern Mendips*

SUGGESTED MAP *OS Explorer 142 Shepton Mallet*

START *Grid reference: ST 635473* **FINISH** *Grid reference: ST 618436*

DOG FRIENDLINESS *Well-behaved dogs can run off lead, except on road*

PARKING *Main pay-and-display, Old Market Road, Shepton Mallet*

PUBLIC TOILETS *Commercial Road car park, Shepton Mallet*

NOTE *Somerbus 776, which stops at Oakhill, leaves from a shelter in Rectory Road, opposite the Great Ostry P&D car park; also from the Cenotaph, near the tourist information centre. Eight buses daily.*

WALK 35 DIRECTIONS

The bus stops at the Oakhill Inn, where you should alight. The walk starts along Fosse Road, passing some 17th-century cottages to Fosse Cottage on the left. Here the track of the Fosse Way sets off on the right. The Fosse Way was the 4th-century equivalent of the M5 motorway, running from the south coast to Lincoln. Ilchester, at the junction with the road to the coast over the Polden Hills, became the local centre of government, with rich civil servants building villas in the countryside around. Shepton Mallet was a Roman industrial town beside the road, and Bath, with its hot springs, was an early motorway service station.

At the first rise the track becomes a sunken path, which is so eroded that the track abandons it for a dog-leg out to the right. It rejoins the Roman line 300yds (274m) further on. Views on the left are

> ### WHILE YOU'RE THERE
> The East Somerset Railway steam trains run for 2.5 miles (4km) along the 'Strawberry Line'. The 1 in 56 (1.8 per cent) gradient is claimed as the steepest restored railway in Britain. 'Oil the Engine and Drive the Train' courses are offered.

across the eastern Mendips. The track runs up to a minor road at the top of the slope.

The direct route through the Woodland Trust's wood ahead involves a steep descent. Those wishing to avoid this can turn right, along the road, for 70yds (64m) to where the signposted 'Fosse Way' continues on the opposite side – divert right for a viewpoint bench at the wood edge. The adventurous can cross directly into the wood, to follow a small path ahead along a buried steel pipe. Drop steeply to the corner of open ground and

SHEPTON MALLET

WHAT TO LOOK OUT FOR

Above Leg Square you pass beneath the walls of the town gaol, in use since 1627. During World War Two, Magna Carta and the Domesday Book were stored here. It was also an American military prison, with executions by firing squad behind its old stone walls.

continues along the wood edge to rejoin the main track.

Roman roads stayed in use for centuries after the Romans' departure; with new roads being built on the foundations of the old, the Fosse Way became, through the ages, the A37. Elsewhere it was useful to define the boundary of a medieval estate: today that line may be a field-edge, and possibly a parish boundary as well. On Beacon Hill the line of the old road is marked by parish boundary stones.

Once out of the wood the wide, tree-lined path continues ahead. Without a map, a straight line is the easiest to survey and lay out on the ground. Often the road is lined up on a convenient sighting point; here, the barrows on Beacon Hill seem to have been the place the Romans aimed for. Modern-day mystics claim the barrows mark the intersection of energy-paths called leys

WHERE TO EAT AND DRINK

The bus from Shepton Mallet passes the Oakhill Brewery. The beer must travel just 300yds (274m) to reach the Oakhill Inn, which is the walk's start point. The King's Arms has been at the end of Garston Street since 1660. Market Place has two pubs and many cafés.

that fly like arrows all over the countryside; the sensitive Celts laid their paths along such lines and the Romans simply built theirs on top.

On reaching a lane, turn left for 150yds (137m), then back right for 250yds (229m). The Fosse Way track continues on the left, just past a stagnant pond. The track rises gradually, then starts to descend with Shepton Mallet in sight ahead. As the descent steepens, bare rock shows in the bed of the trackway. Pass a concrete shed on the right to a fenced gas-board hut, ignore the path off right here, but after another 200yds (183m) comes a stile on the right, with a viaduct ahead.

Cross a field towards the viaduct, passing to the right of a hollow ash tree, then bearing left towards the right-hand of two stiles. A path leads on under the viaduct and across the end of a street into a walled path, with a glimpse into the Jubilee Gardens on the right. Emerge through a small car park.

Turn right past a Georgian brewery and 20th-century cider works; go under an overhead pipe and turn left at a 'Babycham' plastic chamois. Weavers' cottages are on the right before Garston Street bends left, then jiggles into the short cul-de-sac Leg Square. This in turn leads into a walled path, with Gaol Lane continuing up to the right above. Turn right on a paved path ('No Bikes') with a filled-in archway on the left, to pass the church, then bear right to reach the market place. From the Market Cross turn left up the High Street for the tourist information centre or keep ahead along an unnamed narrow street to Great Ostry car park.

Catching the Burrow Mump on the Levels

A gentle wander around the Somerset Levels near Burrowbridge leading up to a hump called a 'mump'.

DISTANCE 5.25 miles (8.4km) **MINIMUM TIME** 2hrs 15min

ASCENT/GRADIENT 150ft (46m) ▲▲▲ **LEVEL OF DIFFICULTY** ✦✦✦

PATHS Tracks, paths, unfrequented field-edges, 2 stiles

LANDSCAPE Flat pasture with ditches and one surprising, small hill

SUGGESTED MAP OS Explorer 140 Quantock Hills & Bridgwater

START / FINISH Grid reference: ST 360305

DOG FRIENDLINESS Good on drove tracks where dogs are separated from livestock by deep ditches

PARKING National Trust car park (free) at Burrow Mump

PUBLIC TOILETS None en route

After the last ice age, around 10–18,000 years ago, this ground was under the sea; in one sense it still is, as the high tide in the Bristol Channel rises up to 20ft (6m) above the fields and ditches. If the sea ever does get back in, it will lap against Glastonbury Tor and make Bridgwater and Burnham reminiscent (albeit in just one sense) of Venice – they will have canals instead of streets.

The draining of this ground started in Roman times, but gathered pace in the early Middle Ages. The three centuries following the Norman conquest (until the Black Death) brought increasing prosperity and security, shown by, among other things, the windmills that sprung up along the Polden Hills. The growing population required more land to be drained for the plough and the cow.

Summer Pasture

The water-meadows around Barrow Mump were first drained by the monks of Glastonbury Abbey in about 1255. They raised walls to keep out the pervasive waters of the River Parrett, to form fertile water-meadows. In winter these would be allowed to flood, their soils enriched by silt from the river. In summer the drained grasslands formed highly fertile grazing land for their cattle, with convenient and effective wet fencing and plenty of fresh drinking water. This agricultural process may give us the origin of 'Sumor Saete' or Somerset, the 'land of summer'.

Drainage was continued through the ages: the King's Sedgemoor Drain, with its complex arrangement of sluices and pumps, was constructed in the 19th century; and managed drainage came to the Huntspill River area during World War Two. Wind pumps were replaced by steam-powered engines and then by the diesel one that may be heard thumping in the distance at the start of the walk. Our route is around the drove tracks and the river barriers, with a final ascent of Burrow Mump for an overall view.

In the days when the surrounding ground was swamp, Burrow Mump was occupied by the local Celtic people against the Romans. In the

BURROW MUMP

Anglo-Saxon era, it was a strongpoint of King Alfred's; he fortified it against Danish raiders coming up the River Parrett. Later it held a Norman castle. Once the surroundings were drained its tactical value decreased, and the present Chapel of St Michael was built by the monks of Athelney Abbey. Even so it remained an obvious strongpoint, and the chapel was held by the Royalists in 1645 after their crushing defeat by Cromwell's New Model Army at the Battle of Langport. It was partially destroyed on that occasion, restored in the 18th century, and has fallen back down again since then.

View from a Hill

The summit, though only raised 100ft (30m) above the sea-level surroundings, commands a wide and interesting view. Half a dozen parish churches can be seen in various directions. The closest of these, looking due north from the Mump, is St Mary's in Westonzoyland, with its square tower. Here captured rebels were imprisoned by government troops after their defeat at the Battle of Sedgemoor in 1685. Closer at hand, the distinctive pattern of droves (tracks) and walls (river barriers, originally 12ft (4m) high and 30ft (9m) wide) can be seen around the water-meadows.

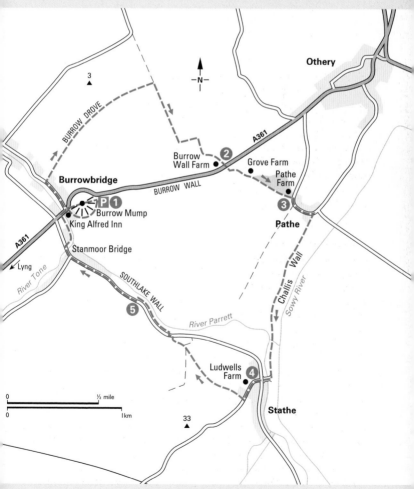

WALK 36 DIRECTIONS

1 A gate leads on to the base of the Mump. Circle the hill's base to the left to a small gate and steps down to the Burrow Bridge. Just before the bridge turn right into Riverside. After 350yds (320m) turn right into Burrow Drove, which becomes a tractor track. On either side and between the fields are deep ditches, coated in bright green pondweed. At a T-junction there's a culvert of 19th-century brick on the left. Here turn right on a new track: it passes round to left of Burrow Wall Farm, to the busy A361.

2 A 'public footpath' sign points to a track opposite. After just 30yds (27m) turn left over a stile. With the bushy Burrow Wall on your right, cross a field to the usually muddy Grove Farm. Go through two gates below a wooded bank rising to continue along fields, to the right of buildings, on the left. At the corner of the second field an awkward rusty gate leads up between brambles to a green track: turn right here to reach a lane near Pathe, a farm.

3 Turn right along the lane, ignoring a track on the right, to reach a side-lane on the right. Here cross a bridge to a hedge-gap

on the right and a very narrow footbridge. Continue through several fields, with a wide ditch on the right. Near by, on the left, is the low banking of Challis Wall, concealing the Sowy River. The ditch on the right gradually gets smaller. When it finally ends bear right to the River Parrett and follow it to a latticework road bridge. Cross this into Stathe.

4 Keep ahead through the village past Ludwells Farm, to reach a kissing gate on the right waymarked 'Macmillan Way'. Follow the right edge of one field to a gatepost; cross to the hedge opposite and follow it round to the left, to a stile. Continue ahead with a hedge on your right, to where a hedged track leads to a road. Turn left, scrambling up the banking, to walk on the Southlake Wall between a road and river.

5 As the road turns away from the river, rejoin it. Once across Stanmoor Bridge you can bear right (if not too nettly) for a river bank path to Burrowbridge. Turn right across the bridge and, this time, climb to the top of Burrow Mump for fine views of Somerset.

Westhay Peatland Reserve

A nature ramble through reconstructed peat marshland, including a brief walk on water.

DISTANCE 4.75 miles (7.7km)	**MINIMUM TIME** 2hrs 15min
ASCENT/GRADIENT 130ft (40m) ▲▲▲	**LEVEL OF DIFFICULTY** +++

PATHS Mostly smooth, level paths and tracks, 2 stiles

LANDSCAPE Reed beds and water-meadows

SUGGESTED MAP OS Explorer 141 Cheddar Gorge

START / FINISH Grid reference: ST 456437

DOG FRIENDLINESS On leads in reserve, can be free on drove tracks

PARKING Free car park at Decoy Pool

PUBLIC TOILETS None en route

NOTE To bypass rough part, follow lane between Points ❹ and ❻

At Westhay Moor the Somerset Wildlife Trust (SWT) is carefully recreating the original peat wetland from a time before drainage and peat cuttings. This involves raising the water table with polythene barriers, and importing sphagnum moss and peatland plants from Cumbria. 'True blanket bog', one of their notices reminds us, 'should wobble when walked on…' And while these rehabilitated peat diggings are very good news for waterfowl and the nightjar, for rare spiders and the bog bush cricket, they are still a long way from the original Somerset moor.

Moor or Morass?

'Moor' is the same as 'mire' or 'morass'; the Saxon word first occurs in the account of King Alfred taking refuge at Muchelney. For the Saxons the moor was a place of mystery and fear. About 1,500 years ago the monster Grendel was the original 'Thing from the Swamp' in the poem of Beowulf. Open water alternated with reed beds and mud. The inhabitants moved around by boat, or by wading, or on stilts. Even if you could see out over the reeds it rarely helped as the mist would come down. And, at nightfall, the will o' the wisp misled you into the unstable mud, just in case you hadn't been swallowed up in it already.

If you did ever get out on to firm land, you were quite likely to be infected with ague or marsh fever. The modern name, 'malaria', reflects its supposed origin in the misty airs of the wetlands. Oliver Cromwell, a fenman from East Anglia, died of malaria. It persisted in the marshes of Essex into the 20th century.

Wet Refuge

For those who knew its ways, the moor was a safe refuge. Iron Age tribes built a village on wooden piles near Glastonbury; the Romans complained of the tribesmen who hid with only their heads above the water. Alfred found safety from the Danes here, as did the monks of Glastonbury.

Wealth in the Wet

The moor was also, in its own way, wealthy. The less wet sections grew a rich summer pasture, fertilised by the silt of the winter floods. It's no coincidence that Britain's most famous cheese comes from the edge of the Levels. The deep, moist soil also grew heavy crops of hemp. Henry VIII made the growing of this useful plant compulsory, as it supplied cordage and sailcloth for the navy. Today, under its Latin name of Cannabis sativa, it is, of course, strictly forbidden. The wetter ground yielded osiers for baskets and reed for thatch; wildfowl and fish; and goosefeather quills for penmen. Fuel was peat, or willow poles from the pollarded trees whose roots supported the ditches. And the rent for this desirable property was often paid in live eels.

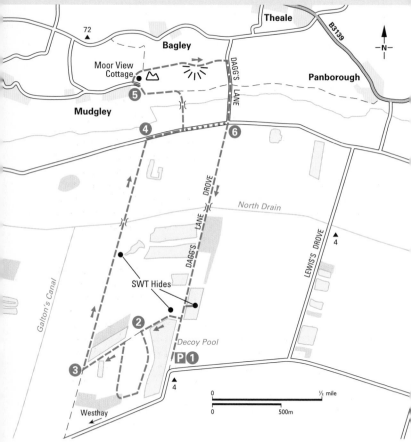

WALK 37 DIRECTIONS

❶ Head into the reserve on a broad track, with Decoy Pool hiding behind reeds on the left. At the end of the lake a kissing gate leads to the SWT hide, with a broad path continuing between high reedbeds. Ignore a gate on the left ('No Visitor Access') but go through a kissing gate 60yds (55m) further on.

❷ A fenced track runs through peat ground, where birches have been felled to recreate blanket bog. The track turns right; now take a kissing gate on the left for

WESTHAY

WALK 37

a path through trees. The path bends right, to leave the wood. After a kissing gate, it continues as a short grassy track. At the end turn left to reach a gate on to the next of the 'droves' or raised trackways through the peatland.

❸ Turn right, passing hides and crossing a bridge over the wide North Drain; the land on each side now comprises water-meadows. The track leads to a lane.

❹ If you wish to omit the field paths above (which are rough, but give a splendid view over the reserve), simply turn right, going along the road for 650yds (594m) to a junction, Point ❻. Otherwise turn right as far as a right-hand bend, and continue for 175yds (160m) to where gates are on both sides of the road. Go through the left-hand one (marked with red paint on the post) and cross to a gate and bridge over a ditch. Follow the left edge of the next field to its corner. Turn left through a gate and then follow a field-edge to a small orchard. Turn right to continue to the end of a tarred lane.

❺ Turn left briefly along the lane to an uphill path to the left of Moor View Cottage – this

becomes overgrown and quite steep – to a stile on the right. Cross the tops of five fields. In the sixth field drop slightly to pass below a farm building. A signpost now points to a field gate just below. Contour across the next field into a small orchard, with a signposted gate on to Dagg's Lane just above. Turn down the lane to the road below.

❻ Directly opposite Dagg's Lane is the track, Dagg's Lane Drove. This runs between meadows then re-enters the reserve, passing between pools left by peat extraction. Look out for a railed path on the left. This leads out excitingly on stilts above the flooded mire to Island Hide. Return from the hide and rejoin the drove track, which quickly leads back to the car park.

Deep Romantic Ebbor Gorge

The small but sublime limestone gorge that inspired Coleridge to write one of his best-known poems, 'Kubla Khan'.

DISTANCE 4.75 miles (7.7km)   MINIMUM TIME 2hrs 30min

ASCENT/GRADIENT 1000ft (305m) ▲▲▲   LEVEL OF DIFFICULTY +++

PATHS Small paths and field-edges, with a rugged descent, 10 stiles

LANDSCAPE Vast view across the Levels, then tight little gorge

SUGGESTED MAP OS Explorer 141 Cheddar Gorge

START / FINISH Grid reference: ST 521484

DOG FRIENDLINESS English Nature asks that dogs to be on leads in reserve

PARKING Lane above Wookey Hole or Wookey Hole's car park below Point ②

PUBLIC TOILETS At Wookey Hole's visitor car park

When Samual Taylor Coleridge (1772–1834) wanted to paint in words the ultimate in sublime landscape, he based his poem not on Snowdonia (which he had visited) but on Somerset. The setting of *Kubla Khan* (1816) is based partly on Culbone Combe, on the Exmoor Coast, and partly on memories of a visit to Wookey Hole and Ebbor. So we have: 'the deep romantic chasm that slanted, down a green hill, athwart a cedern covert; a savage place!' While down at Wookey Hole: 'Alph, the sacred river ran, through caverns measureless to man…'

To the writers and painters of the Romantic period, a landscape could be merely beautiful – or it could be sublime. A scene that's 'sublime' goes far beyond the merely pretty: it induces awe and even terror. It stills the noisy chattering mind, to the point of breaking through into the 'divine Reality' that lies behind the world. Today most of us don't believe in the divine Reality, and aren't driven to sort our views into categories and seek out the sublime. And yet it is possible top experience it on Glastonbury Tor at sunset (see Walk 30) and at midnight on the Quantocks even while staring down on some very 21st-century streetlights.

Ornamental Vision

It's interesting to compare *Kubla Khan* with Stourhead Garden (see Walk 31): the walls and towers are there; the incense-bearing trees; even the domed shapes of the buildings. Stourhead's designer, Henry Hoare, wasn't copying the poem, it's just that he and Coleridge sought the same thing.

The third category of scenery was picturesque. This is one that's arranged correctly, with foreground, middleground, and a hill wall shutting off the end. The foreground should have some ornamental peasants or brigands, from whom a carefully placed river or lane leads the eye into the scene.

Coleridge did pronounce 'Kubla Khan' to rhyme with 'Measureless to man'. We know this from a letter of Dorothy Wordsworth's where she puns on 'Kubla Khan' and 'watering Khan'. Wordsworth himself mocked those who go walking for the sake of the view – the 'craving for a prospect', as he called it. But Ebbor Gorge is impressive whatever its landscape category.

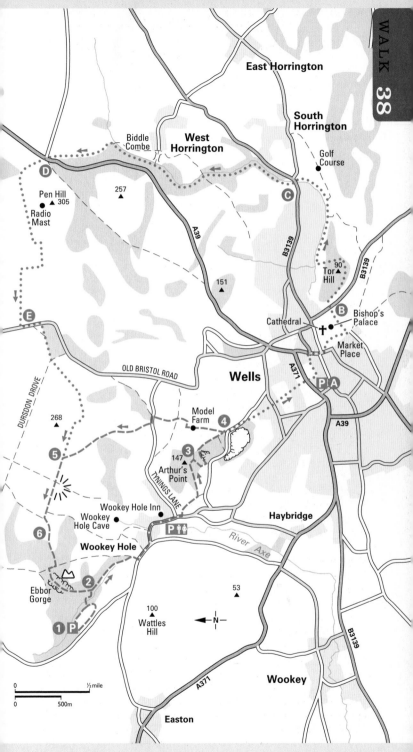

East Horrington

South Horrington

Biddle Combe

West Horrington

Golf Course

D

Pen Hill ▲ 305
Radio Mast

257 ▲

A39

C

B3139

151 ▲

90 Tor ▲ Hill

B3139

B Bishop's Palace

Cathedral ✝

E

OLD BRISTOL ROAD

Market Place

Wells

A371

P A

A39

268 ▲

Model Farm **4**

5

147 ▲ **3**
Arthur's Point

TYNINGS LANE

Haybridge

Wookey Hole Inn
Wookey Hole Cave ●

P 🚻

River Axe

6

Wookey Hole

53 ▲

2

Ebbor Gorge

100 Wattles Hill

← N →

1 P

Wookey

B3139

0 ½ mile
0 500m

A371

Easton

WALK 38 DIRECTIONS

1 From the noticeboard at the top end of the car park descend a stepped path. After a clearing, turn left, signposted 'The Gorge'. The wide path crosses the stream to another junction.

2 Turn right, away from the gorge down the valley to a road. Turn left, to pass through Wookey Hole village. At its end the road bends right; take a kissing gate on the left with a 'West Mendip Way' post. After two more kissing gates turn left up a spur to a stile and the top of Arthur's Point.

3 Bear right for 60yds (55m) into woods again. The path now bears right to a stile. Go down left to a kissing gate back into the wood. At once, and before the lime kiln just ahead, turn up left between boulders to pass between high quarry crags. Bear right along the wood foot to join a short track ahead. It leads to a four-track junction with a waymarker post standing in a stone plinth.

4 Turn sharp left, on to tarred track that bends right then left through Model Farm, to Tynings Lane. Turn left for 85yds (78m) to a signposted stile on the right. Go up with a fence on your right, then bear left to a gate with a stile. Go straight up the next field, aiming for a gateway below the

top left corner with tractor ruts running into it. A track leads up through a wood and a field. From the gate at its top slant upwards in the same direction to another gate next to a stile 100yds (91m) below the field's top left corner.

5 A small path runs along the tops of three fields with a long view across the Levels away to your left. With a stile on the right and a gate and horse trough in front, turn downhill keeping the fence on your right; follow it to a stile leading into the Ebbor Gorge Nature Reserve.

6 A second stile leads into a wood. At a junction with a red arrow and sign marked 'Car Park' pointing forward, turn right into the valley and go down it – this narrows to an exciting, rocky gully. At the foot of the gorge turn right, signposted 'Car Park'. You are now back at Point **2** of the outward walk. After crossing a stream turn left at a T-junction to the wood edge, and back right to the car park.

Wells and Ebbor Gorge

A walk of twice the length, taking in the gorge, and England's smallest city.

See map and information panel for Walk 38

DISTANCE 10.5 miles (16.7km)	**MINIMUM TIME** 4hrs 45min
ASCENT/GRADIENT 1,457ft (450m) ▲▲▲	**LEVEL OF DIFFICULTY** ✦✦✦
PATHS Two wooded combes and a high hillside	

WALK 39 DIRECTIONS
(Walk 38 option)

From Point ❹ of Walk 38, follow West Mendip Way ahead down the lane. Where it bends left at a white house, keep ahead on a track that becomes a tarred path down into Wells. Cross the A371, then turn left on a path that becomes Lovers Walk Lane. Where it bends left, wiggle right then left to a road, then turn right into a 20mph zone. Bear left into Sadler Street, where an arch on the left leads to the cathedral. Turn right to pass through the Penniless Porch to the market place, but at once take another arch left to the Bishop's Palace. Turn right and go round two sides of the moat to the busy B3139, Point ❸.

Cross to the lane at the base of Tor Hill. The path climbs steps to a strip of open grassland. Once under trees again, continue for 75yds (69m) to a gate on the left. Now in another open strip, follow a broken wall on the left to a stile into woods. Go all the way down to a stream at the hill foot. Turn right, following the edge of Wells, with first rugby pitches and then a golf course on your right, to emerge on Bath Road, Point ❸.

Cross to a rusty gate with a footpath sign. The path heads

to the right, ascending Biddle Combe. After 1.5 miles (2.4km) a small lime kiln on the right stands below a stream junction. The main path crosses the left-hand stream and goes up beside it. After a gate out of the wood, keep trees on your left to reach the A39, Point ❸.

Cross to a stone stile. Bear right to join a fence, contouring round Pen Hill below the radio mast. Pass just outside one of the support cables to a stile. Walk left, round three sides of the next field, to a similar stile. Continue ahead with a wall on your left to the Old Bristol Road, Point ❸. Turn left to a bend, then right, into the wooded lane 'Dursdon Drove'. At the wood end bear left on the track marked 'Rookham View'. At a cattle grid bear left (signpost) below farm buildings, then bear up right to a stile at the hill crest. Continue to walk along the slope top, to a gate and stile, Point ❺ on Walk 38.

Cheddar Gorge

A circuit around Somerset's most impressive natural feature and beside the home of its gorgeous cheese.

DISTANCE *3.5 miles (5.7km)* MINIMUM TIME *2hrs 15min*

ASCENT/GRADIENT *1,000ft (305m)* ▲▲▲ LEVEL OF DIFFICULTY +++

PATHS *Stony and sometimes steep and slippery, 3 stiles*

LANDSCAPE *Crag tops and woods*

SUGGESTED MAP *OS Explorer 141 Cheddar Gorge*

START / FINISH *Grid reference: ST 462536*

DOG FRIENDLINESS *Open land, but care needed near cliff edges*

PARKING *Pay-and-display at Cliff Street, Cheddar village, just outside Cheddar Gorge*

PUBLIC TOILETS *Toilets at car park, and at show caves*

WALK 40 DIRECTIONS

From the car park turn right, across a roundabout and over the river to the entrance to the gorge road. This looks more like a fairground than a public highway: indeed it has been a fairground since early Victorian times. Ignoring it for now, bear right into Lippiatt and go up this steep lane for 80yds (73m). Steps on the left lead up to another lane. Go up this to a signed bridleway on the left into woods. At the top is a metal viewpoint tower: it gives a fine view into the gorge, and out to the sea, the distant Quantocks and the Exmoor coast.

A wide path runs uphill, close to the edge of the gorge. Steps arriving from the left are 'Jacob's Ladder', a Victorian attraction whereby visitors to the show caves paid to walk up on to a public footpath. Through a metal kissing gate, now, the path is clear, but the well-trodden limestone becomes very slippery when it's damp. On the left are various viewpoints overlooking the gorge. Careful – King Edmund of England narrowly escaped falling over the edge when hunting up here in the year AD 941, and he wasn't the last.

At the highest point of the path ignore gates on the right but continue between fence and gorge. The path descends quite steeply through a wood to a kissing gate. After a short level stretch it continues down through the wood – this can be muddy and slippery – to the gorge road.

A path ahead continues into the Blackrock Nature Reserve, but the Gorge Walk turns left down

WHAT TO LOOK OUT FOR

In early summer you may find the Cheddar pink. This is a close relative of the garden pink and looks very like it – they are both Dianthus. Its single, fragrant flower grows out of cracks in the limestone around the gorge – and nowhere else in Britain.

the roadside for 200yds (180m) to a waymarked path that climbs through the woods on the right.

After an initially steep ascent it turns left up a long flight of wood-and-earth steps. It continues with a fence on its right and the gorge on its left, gently downhill through thorn scrub that's adorned in autumn with old man's beard. The whiskery seed heads appear in autumn; in spring the flower is called travellers' joy.

At a junction a stile on the left is a side-path running down to the National Trust's (NT) viewpoint. This path descends steeply to an exposed slope above crags: a sensible sign suggests that dogs and children should be closely controlled, and the place should be avoided when very wet or by those with flat-soled shoes. It does give a fine outlook on the gorge mouth and the rock faces opposite.

From the NT viewpoint return over the stile to the path junction and turn left. Head downhill for 250yds (229m). Turn right, away from the gorge, to pass a gate in a wall with a view over Cheddar.

Cheddar is, of course, doubly famous, not only for its gorge but also for its cheese. Cheddar cheese does not have holes in (that's Emmental, from Switzerland) but Cheddar's holes did originally

have cheese in: they were stored underground where the temperature is a chill-cabinet 4°C (39°F) all the year round. The particular process of 'cheddaring' consists of slicing up the curd at a crucial moment, placing it in layers and letting it slump – much the same as what's happened to the limestone strata overhead. The process is fairly easily reproduced on an industrial scale, so that we now have New Zealand Cheddar, Orkney Cheddar, and Cheddar from everywhere in-between. However, authentic, hand-made Cheddar is available at Cheddar Gorge and is considerably tastier than the orange lumps vacuum wrapped in plastic found on supermarket shelves.

Go past (not through) the gate to a stile at the wall corner. The path goes down under trees with a broken wall on its right, then passes through the wall at a kissing gate. At the first houses of Cheddar turn sharp left into a walled path. At the tarred driveway of Cufic House turn left to arrive among the shops and attractions of Cheddar Gorge near the tourist information centre.

Turn right, into a path forbidden to cyclists. It passes behind a mill pool, then runs along the foot of a wood, with a rare chance for the observant to glimpse the extinct sabre-tooth tiger. Rejoin the main road through the gorge at the toilets, and head down past (or via) the tea rooms and snack shops to the car park.

Straight to the Parrett's Mouth

No cliffs or crashing waves — a coastal walk to heighten your understanding of flatlands and mud.

DISTANCE 4.5 miles (7.2km)	**MINIMUM TIME** 1hr 45min
ASCENT/GRADIENT Negligible ▲▲▲	**LEVEL OF DIFFICULTY** ✦✦✦

PATHS Town paths, wide, surfaced track and fields, 16 stiles

LANDSCAPE Level ground, mudflats and sea

SUGGESTED MAP OS Explorer 153 Weston-super-Mare

START / FINISH Grid reference: ST 305455

DOG FRIENDLINESS Good, since half of walk is along open shoreline

PARKING Street parking at Huntspill church

PUBLIC TOILETS Just off-route in Highbridge

The walk's start point was formerly several miles out to sea, with the shoreline at the foot of the Polden Hills (see Walk 20). Since the last Ice Age the tidal flow up and down the Bristol Channel has created the bank of clay mud on which you are now standing. Huntspill church, and the nearby houses, are built on Plymor Hill. At just 2ft (60cm) high, this must be the lowest hill in the country; even so, during the floods of 1981, the people who live here were glad of the extra altitude.

Managing Mud

Humans have drained the land behind this mud ridge to form the Somerset Levels and moors (see Walk 37). The watercourses that drain all that fertile 'summer land' – the Kings Sedgemoor Drain, the Parrett itself – would also let the sea back in at every high tide, and so they must be closed off. We shall pass the barrier that closes the River Brue in the course of the walk. On the left you pass a concrete pill box, a coastal defence from World War Two. On the other side, across the River Brue, you'll see a defence built against an enemy even more dangerous than the Germans: the sea itself. The Environment Agency, currently responsible for keeping the sea out of Britain, is coming to realise that such Canute-like and unsubtle ways of fighting the ocean are going to become less and less effective as global warming brings a rise in the sea, more autumn storms, and higher rainfall to swell the rivers behind. In November 2000 the Deputy Prime Minister, John Prescott, was very impressed by a Dutch system of overflow areas: deliberately letting floodwaters into certain areas for pumping out afterwards. 'Britain needs such a system' he declared – but in the Somerset Levels, Britain already has it.

Hinkley Point

On the other side of the estuary stands what is either a noble and striking focus for the rather flat landscape, or a sinister horror; which of the two you see depends largely on which newspaper you believe. Is the nuclear power station at Hinkley Point an environmental nightmare, spreading radioactive pollutants and threatening us all with cancer and worse? Or is it part of the only medium-term solution to carbon dioxide emissions and global warming? However it is probably both of these things.) There is a certain irony in the fact that within its fence the Hinkley Point power station harbours a small, but valuable, nature reserve protecting the home of 29 different types of butterfly and the rare bee orchid, and is a haven for the nightingale as well.

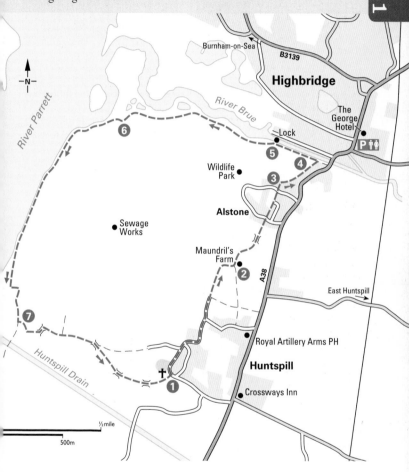

WALK 41 DIRECTIONS

❶ Head away from the church with houses on your right and trees on your left (with the sea behind them). The street, Church Road, bends right then back left: at the next bend keep ahead in Longlands Lane, which becomes hedged path between ditches. Join a concrete track that bends right to ugly Maundril's Farm.

❷ Turn left on a waymarked footpath between huge sheds. Cross a track to an overgrown path ending at a stile, and turn half right to cross a field to a footbridge. A fenced path leads to a street and continues beyond it. It passes along the end of a second street, to reach a third.

❸ Again a tarred path continues opposite, to emerge into a field.

WHERE TO EAT AND DRINK

The Crossways is an old coaching inn with good food, real ales and considerable atmosphere. Dogs (on leads) are accepted and families are welcome. There is also the Royal Artillery Arms and the George Hotel in Highbridge.

WHILE YOU'RE THERE

Secret World wildlife rescue centre, at East Huntspill, is open to visitors on selected weekends only – their orphaned baby hedgehogs, deer and squirrels need peace and quiet most of the time – so check their website for details and opening times.

A fenced-off way runs round the edge of the field to an overgrown path ending at a stile. Continue along the right-hand edge of the field to its corner.

④ Here a walled way leads out to the right: take this if you wish to cross the bridge to visit Highbridge. Opposite the burnt-out Highbridge Inn is a memento of the former seaport: a handsome Victorian warehouse in brick and stone. (Toilets are found across the roundabout in a car park on the right.) The main walk continues from Point ④ along the field-edge near the River Brue, with its banks of brown mud, to reach the sea lock.

⑤ Bear left for 30yds (27m) to a stile, and follow a path on the flood bank alongside the tidal river. As the banking reaches the sea, a stile and gate on the right lead on to the concrete top of more sea defences.

⑥ Follow what is in effect a concrete track along the shoreline for a mile (1.6km). Here the limestone blocks, broken up by the sea, have fairly easy-to-find fragments of large ammonites (see Walk 12). Where the concrete disappears under grass bear left to a gate, and cross the earth barrier to reach a tarred lane. After 150yds (137m) this bends inland to a lay-by, with a stile on the left just beyond.

⑦ Cross a stile here, and head towards Huntspill church on a faint field path with a hedge and ditch on your left. Cross a footbridge on the left – here field boundaries are made of water sometimes backed up by a hedge. Turn right alongside the hedge and ditch to join a track. After 300yds (274m) watch out for a footbridge on the right. Turn left until blocked by a ditch, then turn right to find a narrow footbridge. Head straight towards the church, over stiles and a footbridge, to enter the churchyard through a kissing gate.

WHAT TO LOOK FOR

Between the sea wall and the sea is salt pasture. Grass isn't the only plant that has managed to occupy this difficult niche, periodically submerged in salt water. Marsh samphire grows out of the perforated blocks of the sea wall. This low plant has fleshy leaves and spreading frothy flowers of greenish yellow. The plant used to be pickled and eaten with fish. Given the amount of human settlement around the Bristol Channel it would be unwise to gather it here.

Over Crook Peak and Wavering Down

A high-level ridge wander in the western Mendips over a lot of geology to Somerset's shapeliest summit.

DISTANCE 6 miles (9.7km)   **MINIMUM TIME** 3hrs

ASCENT/GRADIENT 900ft (274m) ▲▲▲   **LEVEL OF DIFFICULTY** +++

PATHS Field-edges, then wide clear paths, 7 stiles

LANDSCAPE Open, grassy hilltop and ridge, and a wood

SUGGESTED MAP OS Explorer 153 Weston-super-Mare

START / FINISH Grid reference: ST 392550

DOG FRIENDLINESS Off-lead, but be aware of horses in woods and on open hill

PARKING On road between Cross and Bleadon, west of Compton Bishop; also street parking in Cross and on A38

PUBLIC TOILETS None en route; nearest at Winscombe

The rock which forms the Mendips, as well as the White Peak and the Yorkshire Dales, used to be known as the Mountain limestone. This name has sadly been abandoned – perhaps after complaints from the non-Mountain limestones of Everest, the Pyrenees and the Eiger... Now called Carboniferous limestone, it was laid down at a time when England was under water and drifting slowly north across the Equator. The next rocks to form on top, as the Carboniferous sea became a swampy river-delta, were the coal measures. A thick layer of coal has in fact eroded off the top of the Mendips and, like the Pennines, the Mendips have a coal field next door.

Comfort Underfoot

In the Pennines the limestone is layered with waterproof gritstone so that dry ground alternates with peat bog. The Mendips are limestone all the way down. This gives a very enjoyable form of walking or (perhaps even better) horse-riding. The grass is cropped short by roe deer and rabbits, and bright in spring with lime-loving wild flowers. The sides drop away in hawthorn scrub and the mildest of craggy bits to a wide, fertile plain. The path along the ridge is fast and easy, and every 20 minutes it peeps down into another wooded hollow. The other side of Somerset, the Quantocks, are a different sort of limestone but give the same delightful walking. Sadly, the Quantocks and the Mendips are small in area. Furthermore, elsewhere in England, or even in the world, there isn't very much of this limestone downland at all.

Geological Crunches

Geologists believe that, oddly, this is the second time around for the Mendips. The continental collision nicknamed 'the Africa Crunch' folded the sea-bottom limestones into mountains of about Ben Nevis height (which isn't very high – Ben Nevis in its prime was Everest height). The soft, coal-like stuff was eroded away and the Mendip Mountains wore down to their present shape in the early dinosaur age. Then Britain sank, and the mountain outlines disappeared under thousands of feet (up to 1,000m) of ocean sediments. The next event, 'the Alpine Crunch', lifted everything up again about 50 million years ago, and since then the topping has gradually worn away to reveal the limestone landscape underneath.

According to this theory, the limestone gorges around the Mendips have formed twice over. The first time, as wadis or desert valleys scoured by flash floods; the second time, under ice age conditions, with the underground waterways frozen. Thus contradictory geological noticeboards explain Burrington Combe (desert wadi) and Cheddar Gorge (Ice Age meltwaters). Given that limestone gorges don't have rivers, they ought not to occur even once; doing it twice, for two different reasons, is good going!

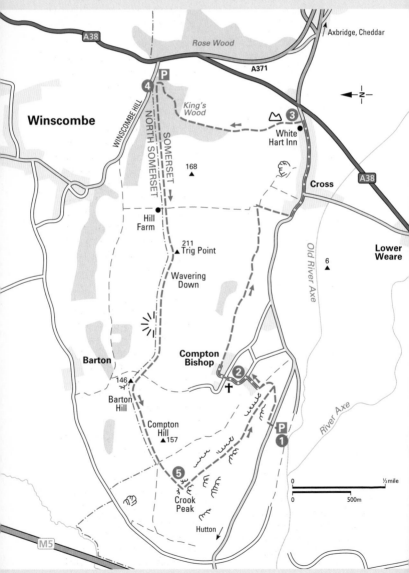

WALK 42 DIRECTIONS

1 Cross the road to a wide gate on the right (not the small gate ahead). A wide path contours round through brambly scrub, crosses the ridge line and drops through a wood and then along its foot to a gate. Just below, a lane leads down into Compton Bishop. Turn left to the church.

2 The lane turns down, before the church, to a crossroads. Take the track opposite and follow it round a bend to its end. You will now contour round the base of the high slope of Wavering Down. Cross a stile, pass through a wrought-iron gate into a narrow paddock, and cross another stile into a large field; keep along the bottom edge of this. At its corner keep ahead over a stile, then across the foot of three more fields. Move 40yds (37m) uphill around a fence corner to another stile on the same level. Follow the long bottom edge

of a field, then cross another under a power line, to a track and turn right, down to the road. Turn left through Cross village.

3 At a 'Give Way 150yds' sign (warning of the A38 ahead) turn left up a steep rocky path. It turns right above a fence, then slants up to rejoin the same fence higher up. It enters woodland, running just above the foot of the wood, through two gates. Now a wide earth path, it finally emerges at the top of the car park located on Winscombe Hill.

4 Turn left, away from the car park, on a broad track, uphill. This rises through King's Wood, then dips slightly to pass the pantiled Hill Farm, before rising to the trig point on Wavering Down. Continue with a wall on your right to cross Barton Hill. In the dip below Crook Peak the wall ends. Waymarkers point to left and right, but keep ahead to climb the slightly crag-topped summit.

5 Turn left and (with the small rocky drop down to your left) head down on to a long gentle ridge – outcrops of limestone poke out through the shallow grass. At a railed barrier turn right on the path back to the car park.

Dolebury Warren

A fine walk through woodland, heathland and an Iron Age hill-fort on the northern rim of the Mendips.

DISTANCE 5.25 miles (8.4km)   MINIMUM TIME 2hrs 30min

ASCENT/GRADIENT 750ft (229m) ▲▲▲   LEVEL OF DIFFICULTY +++

PATHS Wide and mostly mud-free, 4 stiles

LANDSCAPE A grassy hilltop rises out of mixed woodland

SUGGESTED MAP OS Explorer 141 Cheddar Gorge

START / FINISH Grid reference: ST 444575

DOG FRIENDLINESS Dogs can run free on Dolebury Warren

PARKING Pull-off near church; street parking in Shipham centre

PUBLIC TOILETS None en route; nearest at Winscombe

Somerset has a lot of Iron-Age forts. It may just be that Somerset has rather a lot of the right sort of hill. These hill-forts were not just defensive structures, but small townships. Inside the summit wall were roundhouses of wattle and daub. Wattle is a woven framework of willow twigs, and its daub is a mixture of clay and straw – the most waterproof daub also has plenty of cow-dung in it. Reed thatch made a cosy roof. The houses were up to 50ft (15m) across with a central fireplace.

'Barbarian' Propaganda

The inhabitants of these hill-forts are the first people about whom we have written records. However, the writers were their enemies, the Romans. The Durotinges, who inhabited Somerset and Dorset, are portrayed, along with the other British tribes, as warlike and savage barbarians. Warlike would seem to be correct. Their settlements, whether hill-forts or the lake village at Glastonbury, were placed so as to be defended. In the case of the hill-forts, they clearly valued the protective wall above having a convenient water supply. And Boudicca, often called Boadicea, chieftain of the Iceni of East Anglia, certainly earned the respect of the Romans even though they eventually defeated her, as they did the Durotinges on Cadbury Castle. 'Savage barbarians', however, is just enemy propaganda.

These were people with a developed civilisation based on farming, fishing and hunting, as well as warfare. At Glastonbury their village on stilts in the marshland is itself illustrates a considerable feat of co-operative working from a very early time. They built log trackways across the peatlands, or paddled home in a canoe hollowed out of a single tree trunk with flint axes and fire.

Iron Age Craft and Culture

They traded with their neighbours; rounded pebbles from Chesil Beach, used as ammunition by slingers, have been found at Ham Hill. They wove baskets and made jewellery of bronze. They appreciated fine, or at least garish, clothing, coloured using plant dyes (madder for red and woad for

DOLEBURY WARREN

blue) and pinned with a bronze brooch at the shoulder. They kept bees, and they made pottery which is still an inspiration to potters of today. At night the roundhouse was lit with rushlights made from the pith of reeds and soaked in mutton fat. And from what we know of Iron Age-type societies in more recent history, they had a rich tradition of story-telling and a detailed knowledge of their own family trees.

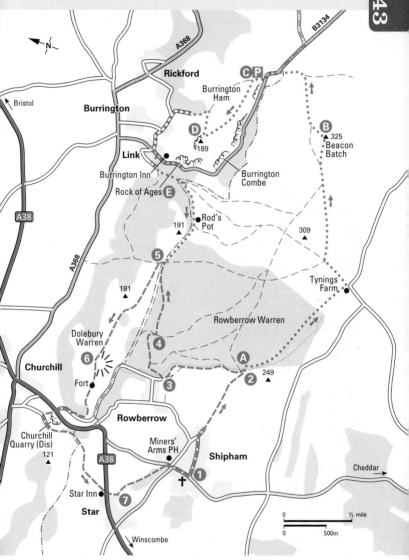

WALK 43 DIRECTIONS

1 From the war memorial crossroads in the centre of Shipham village head uphill on Hollow Road (signposted 'Rowberrow'). At the top of the street bear right into Barn Pool, and at its end turn right again into Lipiatt Lane. At the lane's top end, keep straight ahead on a path with a waymarker for Cheddar, to descend a sunken path to a stream.

2 Just before the stream turn left on a path marked 'Rowberrow'. Stay to the left of the stream (ignoring a fork off to the right) – the path becomes a track. After passing three houses and a lime kiln, at the start of tarmac, turn right into the forest at a noticeboard, 'Rowberrow Warren'.

3 The track bends to the right, climbing. At the corner of an open field turn left into a smaller track that descends gently with this field above on its right. At a junction keep ahead, uphill, for 35yds (32m) then turn left on a forest track with a bridleway sign.

4 After 350yds (320m) bear left down the gradually shrinking track, soon with young spruce (Christmas trees) above on the right. Where it joins a stony track below, bear right on the stony track, with a wall to your left. At a T-junction turn left for 90yds (82m) to a gate on the left with a National Trust sign.

5 Follow the grassy ridgeline ahead, along a line of thorn trees, then passing along the left side of a fenced enclosure of scrubland. Bear right ('Limestone Link' waymarker) to pass to the right of a tall pine clump. Emerge on to more open grassland with wide views. The highest point of the ridge is the rim of the huge Dolebury hill-fort.

6 A green track runs down through the fort and into the woods below. It bends left, then back right, to emerge at a gate on to tarred lanes. Take the lane on the right, down to the A38. Cross to a signposted bridleway: this leafy path with a bedrock bottom rises to a lane. Turn up left – the hummocky ground on the left consists of broken stones from the disused Churchill Quarry below. Ignore turnings to left and right and follow the enclosed track down to Star.

7 Cross the A38 on to a grass track to a stile, and go up the grassy spur above. Keep up next to some trees on your right to a stile, and pass to the right of a football pitch, to find a short path out to the edge of Shipham. Turn right, to the village centre.

Batch and Combe

A longer and more demanding option, to the summit of the Mendips.

See map and information panel for Walk 43

DISTANCE *9 miles (14.5km)* **MINIMUM TIME** *4hrs 30min*
ASCENT/GRADIENT *1,500ft (457m)* ▲▲▲ **LEVEL OF DIFFICULTY** +++

WALK 44 DIRECTIONS (Walk 43 option)

The cap of sandstone that lies on the Mendip limestone means that Beacon Batch is more like Exmoor or the Pennines, with peat, gorse and heather. Burrington Combe was formed as a rainwater gulch in hot desert conditions, and is still much drier than Beacon Batch.

At Point **A** (Point **2** of Walk 43) cross the stream and turn right on a bridleway that gradually rises up the left-hand side of its little valley to Tynings Farm. After a grey and silver shed turn left on a fenced-in track to the heathland of Beacon Batch. Ignoring bridleway waymarkers, turn right on a path that slants gradually up. Fork right on to a hollowed out red-earthed path for the final 350yds (320m) to the summit trig point, Point **B**.

Bear left (second exit, in roundabout terms) on a descending path that at a lone birch tree joins another to slant down to the right. At the corner of the open heath turn down to the B3134 and follow as it descends to a car park, Point **C**.

Take the rocky bridleway just above and to the right of the road. After 200yds (183m) a footpath turns off left along the crest of Burrington Ham. After 0.5 mile (800m) reach a rocky outcrop, Point **D**.

Turn right below the outcrop on a slanting path down into woods. Where it levels off, turn sharp left to join a bridleway. This joins a lane; keep ahead to reach the B3134 at Link. Turn left alongside the road to pass the Burrington Inn and admire Burrington Combe and the Rock of Ages, Point **E**, where the Revd John Toplady sheltered from a thunderstorm in a cleft that looks barely waterproof and subsequently wrote the famous hymn. (He didn't find the drier and deeper Plumley's Den, near by, but 'Den of Ages' isn't nearly as good a hymn title.)

Return along the B3134, bearing left into a tarred track and turning up left just before a house on a short but steep path. Turn left just before a house in the lane above, which, after concrete gate posts, becomes a track. It passes to left of Link Bungalow, then bends gradually right, with fence and woodland on its right. A small pothole, Rods Pot, is alongside the track as it drops into a valley with conifers over on the left. After a gate into woodland, the bridleways divide. Here, fork right for 90yds (82m) to a gate on the left with a National Trust sign – Point **5** on Walk 43.

Through Geological Time in the Avon Gorge

WALK 45

A fascinating walk through a famous gorge with a chance to see one of Brunel's masterpieces.

DISTANCE *4.25 miles (6.8km)*   MINIMUM TIME *2hrs*

ASCENT/GRADIENT *350ft (107m)* ▲▲▲   LEVEL OF DIFFICULTY +++

PATHS *Wide and mostly waymarked, one steep section, no stiles*

LANDSCAPE *Wooded slopes, tidal riverside, and a gorge*

SUGGESTED MAP *OS Explorer 154 Bristol West & Portishead*

START / FINISH *Grid reference: ST 553740*

DOG FRIENDLINESS *Dogs can be off lead throughout*

PARKING *At Leigh Woods*

PUBLIC TOILETS *Across Clifton Bridge, near observatory*

WALK 45 DIRECTIONS

A noticeboard opposite the car park shows two waymarked trails, one of which, the Purple Trail, is upgraded to wheelchair-friendly smoothness. This walk links parts of the two trails with the riverside walk along the famous gorge.

Start from the noticeboard on the Red Trail. This begins as a wide earth path towards the river. After 50yds (46m) the red and purple trail bears right. In another 90yds (82m) turn left on the Red Trail as the Purple Trail continues ahead.

The wide path runs under beech trees, past a shelter that is roofed with shingles (wooden tiles). At a T-junction with the wood dropping away ahead, the Red Trail turns left, heading up along the rim of a wooded combe. After 110yds (100m) gently downhill, where a red waymarker points ahead, bear right, into the combe, and turn down its floor for 200yds (183m). The trail then turns left on to a terrace path with glimpses of the river below. The sound that

could be the roar of the Avon's rapids is in fact the traffic on the A4 on the far bank.

After 300yds (274m), at a point with a view ahead along the river, it bears right on a smaller path past a picnic table. The path slants down across a shallow combe to a T-junction with fir trees. Here follow blue markers (a cycle trail). At its foot is the River Avon, where you turn right – your route now follows the Avon upstream on a wide riverside path for 1.5 miles (2.4km).

The river possibly predates the low hills it runs through. The land was pushed up into a dome as a distant effect of continental movements elsewhere: Africa banging against Spain 300 million years ago. As the land rose the river carved its way down to form

---

WHERE TO EAT AND DRINK

The pleasant George Inn at Abbot's Leigh has a family garden, and serves good food and traditional ales.

WHILE YOU'RE THERE

A short diversion – 2 miles (3.2km) out and back – will take you on to the Clifton Bridge itself, and the Clifton Bridge Museum at its near end. Here you can see pictures, models and explanations of the bridge's construction. If this fires you with enthusiasm for I K Brunel – as well it may – you could visit the SS Great Britain and Temple Meads Station, both in Bristol city centre.

the gorge. The doming caused by the 'Africa Crunch' can be seen in the cliff faces opposite. The left-hand crags are reddish sandstone of Devonian age, some of the oldest rocks in Somerset. These have also been used in the railway wall alongside your path. Upstream, you pass opposite a high wall of pale brown limestone, its strata dipping steeply to the right. As we head upstream, we are also passing forward through the geological ages, passing from the Devonian to the Carboniferous roughly 50 million years later.

But geological studies are distracted by the impressive Clifton Bridge, now almost overhead. Some 220yds (201m) before the bridge a rock-buttress opposite is studded with metal pins to stop it falling on the A4. Here turn off to the right, passing under a railway bridge beside a monster Buddleia bush. A rather rough path goes up the floor of Nightingale Valley. Here your feet may feel a practical consequence of shifting from the Devonian to the Carboniferous: the limestone bedrock forms a particularly sticky sort of mud.

At the valley top a gap stile ahead leads out on to a street; a left turn in this street (North Road) would take you out on to the Clifton Bridge (0.75 mile, 1.2km). Alternatively, the Blue Trail on the right can provide a quick return (0.75 mile/1.2km) to the car park. However, our route turns sharp right before the gap stile, on to a path marked 'No Bikes'. Fork right near a house to stay alongside the drop into Nightingale Valley on the right. The earth path passes through the earthworks of Stokeleigh Camp, to reach a viewpoint overlooking the river.

From this viewpoint turn sharp left, alongside wooden railings protecting the drop on the right. After 250yds (229m) the path forks; bear right, to pass through the earthwork to a small pond on the left. Turn left on the Purple Trail, with the ditch and earth wall of the hill-fort on your left. After 200yds (183m) another purple waymarker points to the right. The trail wiggles through a wall gap, and in another 80yds (73m) forks left at a bench. It then runs straight through the wood, and arrives at the tarred access track with speed bumps, close to the car park.

WHAT TO LOOK OUT FOR

On the inland side of the riverside path you'll spot 18th-century mooring bollards of the Society of Merchant Venturers. Bristol superseded Bridgwater as the most convenient safe harbour on the West England coastline, and so became Britain's second city. If you wanted raisins or sugar in the 17th century, you sent to Bristol for them. A well-maintained ship is 'Bristol fashion' and a leading brand of sherry appears to come from Bristol rather than Spain. The port was also a centre of the slave trade.

Goblin Combe and Corporation Woods

A forest full of rockfaces gives a walk of crag tops and hollows.

DISTANCE *5.25 miles (8.4km)*   MINIMUM TIME *2hrs 20min*

ASCENT/GRADIENT *400ft (122m)* ▲▲▲   LEVEL OF DIFFICULTY ✦✦✦

PATHS *Tracks and paths, one steep-stepped ascent, 2 stiles*

LANDSCAPE *Wooded hollows and open pasture above*

SUGGESTED MAP *OS Explorer 154 Bristol West & Portishead*

START / FINISH *Grid reference: ST 459653*

DOG FRIENDLINESS *Freedom in Cleeve Woods but lead essential in Corporation Wood (vermin traps)*

PARKING *Goblin Combe car park (free) at Cleeve Hill Road (turn off A370 at Lord Nelson pub)*

PUBLIC TOILETS *None en route*

Walkers in the Lake District or Wales become familiar with the effects of glaciers on the landscape: U-shaped valleys, corrie hollows, and so on. Glaciers never reached Somerset, but the county has certain so-called 'peri-glacial' landforms, caused by the permafrosted tundra climate just next door to the ice cap. Where, for example, is the fair-sized river that carved out the rocky Goblin Combe?

This is limestone country, and the water flows under the ground. But in the ice age times the underground was frozen, and the summer meltwaters could flow across the surface and make gorges. Ice age freeze-and-thaw action in the rocks has broken off large boulders, which lie on either side of the track, and smaller pieces which form scree at the crag foot.

'Adventure Climbing'

Goblin Combe's rocks provide short but entertaining climbs. Notices forbidding climbing are to some extent a legal fiction. The law as it stands doesn't understand the self-reliant ethos of rock-climbing; and the landowner could, in theory, be sued by a fallen climber. Nevertheless, venturing on to the rocks without the proper skill and equipment is both stupid and dangerous. Unlike many limestone cliffs in Somerset you will not – or at least should not – see bolt anchors drilled into Goblin's rocks. Rock climbers and the British Mountaineering Council have designated this an 'adventure climbing' area, where such aids to easier and safer climbing are not seen as sporting.

Limestone Heath Paradox

Above the crags and treetops is limestone meadow with many wild flowers. Here is also limestone heath – a paradox to gardeners, who know that heathers hate lime. Once again, the answer lies in the ice age, when acidic, sandy soil from elsewhere blew in on the sub-zero winds. Sadly, the airy openness of the crag-top meadow is spoilt by the procession of aircraft taking off from Bristol International Airport.

Most of the woodland in Goblin Combe is of ash trees – typical in the Mendips, but relatively rare in Britain as a whole, where the natural succession arrives at oak, birch or (in the mountains) Scots pine. The ash, however, wins out over its rivals on this thin limestone soil. Later in the walk, Corporation Wood is of beeches. Climax woodland (that is a wood that has no further tendency to evolve into some other sort of wood) is composed of a tree species that throws sufficient shade to suppress others. Beeches are particularly good at this, and so Corporation Wood is open and spacious between the smooth tree trunks. Below, there's an occasional 'etiolated' (made pale for want of light) evergreen such as holly, yew or ivy. Also, of course, the young seedlings of the beech wood itself, specially adapted to the heavy shade of their parents.

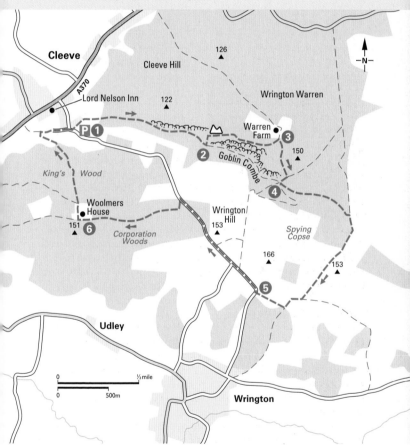

WALK 46 DIRECTIONS

1 From the parking area turn right into Plunder Street and bear left past the Goblin Combe Environmental Centre to pass through a gateway marked

'Footpath to Wrington only'. An earth track leads up the combe bottom, with grey crags above on the left.

2 After 0.75 mile (1.2km) the track passes through a wall gap.

Here, turn left up steep wooden steps. At the slope top the path bends right, and runs alongside a broken wall. On the right, yew trees conceal the drop beyond, but after 100yds (91m) the path bears right, through a gap in the wall, to reach the open crag top. Turn left for 270yds (247m) through a gate and along a clearing. After another 100yds (91m) is another gate. A green track leads down to a noticeboard near outbuildings of Warren Farm. (The noticeboard indicates 'You are here' but actually you're slightly further to the south…)

WHILE YOU'RE THERE

Nearby Clevedon is an elegant seaside resort. Its Victorian pier is one of the finest surviving and is 1,100ft (335m) long. If you time it correctly you can step from the pier on to the paddle steamers, *Waverley* or *Balmoral*, for a trip to the new Severn Bridge.

WHAT TO LOOK OUT FOR

The rare moonwort fern grows under the yew trees of Goblin Combe. Its ragged-looking fronds are 2–8 inches (5–20cm) long with brown spore structures rather like dry seed heads. Alchemists believed this fern would help them turn mercury into silver.

❸ Turn right on a green track gently uphill. As it bends right, fork down left on a greener track to the floor of a shallow combe. Turn right for 110yds (100m) to a junction of combes and tracks.

❹ Turn sharp left, past tree trunk obstructions, on a green track in the bottom of a new combe. With the wood edge visible ahead, bear left to a barrier and turn right in the track beyond. This runs along the wood edge. Sudden loud noises here may be jays in the

WHERE TO EAT AND DRINK

The Lord Nelson, on the A370, could be described as a 'cheap steak' inn; but it does have a pleasant beer garden and an indoor play area for children.

wood (or aeroplanes taking off!). After the corner of Spying Copse the track runs into open pasture. It turns right and then left, and after another 100yds (91m) watch out for a kissing gate on the right-hand side; a grassy way leads across a field to a lane (Wrington Hill).

❺ Turn right for 0.75 mile (1.2km), and, just after the road leaves the beeches of Corporation Woods, turn back left on a track through a gate marked 'Congresbury Woodlands'. The house on the left has an unusual attempt at topiary (tree-clipping) in bay leaves. After a bungalow on the right-hand side the track descends to Woolmers House.

❻ After passing the kennels, turn right on a waymarked track, to go through a gate into King's Wood. The broad path ahead leads to a waymarked footbridge. After another 35yds (32m) bear left with the waymarkers. The path runs down to reach a stile at the foot of the wood. Bear slightly left towards a gate (with a track just beyond), but turn right along the foot of the field. A stile on the left leads to a tarred lane and the car park.

Hunstrete and Compton Dando

Serenity enjoyed in a rich landscape nestling between the busy cities of Bristol and Bath.

DISTANCE *6.25 miles (10.1km)* **MINIMUM TIME** *3hrs 30min*

ASCENT/GRADIENT *700ft (213m)* ▲▲▲ **LEVEL OF DIFFICULTY** ✦✦✦

PATHS *Tracks, field paths, woodland paths, and byways, 11 stiles*

LANDSCAPE *Rolling farmland with plantations and small streams*

SUGGESTED MAP *OS Explorer 155 Bristol & Bath*

START / FINISH *Grid reference: ST 632644*

DOG FRIENDLINESS *Freedom in some woods and on tracks fenced off from farmland*

PARKING *Street parking near bridge in Woollard; also opposite pub in Compton Dando (Point ⑥)*

PUBLIC TOILETS *None en route*

Somerset as an entity is older than England itself; it came into existence as a kingdom of the Saxons after their defeat of King Arthur. This book conforms to the ancient boundaries established, perhaps by Alfred himself, in the 9th century. Local Government reorganisation in 1974 split off a section and called it 'Avon' – the people of Somerset were not pleased. Destruction-of-Somerset Day happened to be 1st April, and to mark this particular All Fools' Day a muffled quarter-peal of Somerset Surprise Major was rung from Yatton church.

Name Game

Local government re-organisation in 1996 largely restored the ancient county. However, this corner remains separate as a unitary authority called Bath and North East Somerset, resulting in the unfortunate acronym, 'BANES'. The other end of Avon has become another unitary authority, North Somerset. The very names of them are an admission that they may be convenient units of government but aren't actually proper places at all. Although it has no striking natural features, 'BANES' does have a character of its own. It can be seen as the final petering-out of the Cotswolds, even if it does lack the Cotswolds' sudden edges – for the most part it's a quiet land of gentle hills, with villages hidden in the occasional small valley. It's rich farming country, with small but bushy woods on the slopes and stream banks too steep for the plough.

Bigoted Views

A remnant of that farming wealth is at Hunstrete, where there's an attractive little angling lake that makes a good picnic spot. It was one of six dug into the grounds of Hunstrete House – a magnificent country mansion of 17 bays with statues to match. It was planned in the 1780s under the influence of Bath's new streets and squares, incomplete in 1797 and already falling down in 1822. Landscaping plans at nearby country houses were even more

135

ambitious and expensive. At Marston Bigot and at Berkley, to improve the view from the windows, they removed and rebuilt a parish church. The authorities charged with making up reasons for footpaths have had to use some imagination. At the start of this walk you'll use the Two Rivers Way: the rivers are Yeo and Chew. From Lord's Wood to Hunstrete you're on the 'Three Peaks Walk': these are not Ben Nevis, Snowdon and Scafell Pike; they aren't even Yorkshire's Whernside, Pen-y-ghent and Ingleborough. They are, in fact, Maes Knoll, Knowle Hill and Blackberry Hill, but none of this will detract from the pleasure of this walk.

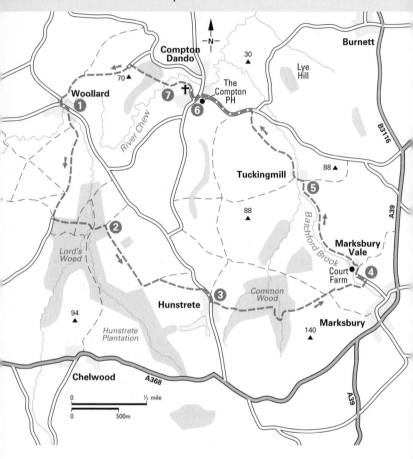

WALK 47 DIRECTIONS

❶ From Woolard's crossroads take the road signposted 'Hunstrete' across the River Chew, then bear right at a 'Circular Walk' sign. The byway is underwater at first, but a path parallels it on the right. At the high point of the byway, where it becomes fully tarred, turn left through a gate into Lord's Wood. A wide path runs downhill, crossing a track, to a pool. Pass around to the left of this, to a waymarker and a track junction. The track opposite leads up to the edge of the wood.

❷ Turn right, and drop to a hidden footbridge under trees. Head uphill, passing the right-hand edge of a plantation, to Pete's Gate beside a corner of Hunstrete Plantation. Turn left to a field gate. Turn right, around the field corner, to go through a gate. Continue along the same hedge, bending right at the field end, to reach a lane at the edge of Hunstrete.

❸ Turn left beside Cottage No 5. Go down the right-hand side of a field to a stile into Common Wood. The track ahead passes through a paintball sports area. After it crosses a stream and bends left, take a signposted green path that rises to the top of the wood. Pass through a small col with a lone ash tree, and keep straight on, down across a field to a short hedged path. Go straight down the left edge of the field to a signpost, and turn right to join a lane at Marksbury Vale.

❹ Turn left towards Court Farm; just before the buildings turn right over a stile, and take the right-hand track for 100yds (91m) to a stile on the left. Pass to the right of the farm buildings to a rough track following Bathford Brook. Head downstream to reach a track at Tuckingmill.

❺ Follow the track past a handsome, 18th-century manor house to a ford. Cross the footbridge and turn right, alongside the stream, which is again the line of an underwater

byway – rejoin it as it emerges. It leads to a road, with Compton Dando 700yds (640m) away on the left.

❻ Turn right into Church Lane, and then go through the lychgate. A stile leads down steps, one of which is a 17th-century gravestone. Turn left behind the mill house and pass to the left of the mill pond, to reach a footbridge over the River Chew.

❼ Bear left into Park Copse. At its top follow the right-hand edge of a field round to a stile. In the lane beyond turn left; it becomes a hedged track and runs past a tiny gorge as it descends to Woollard.

Into the Hollows Around Wellow

A green valley walk, where Cotswold melds into Mendip, tracing a legacy of abandoned industry and failed technology.

DISTANCE *6.5 miles (10.4km)*   MINIMUM TIME *3hrs 30min*

ASCENT/GRADIENT *750ft (228m)* ▲▲▲   LEVEL OF DIFFICULTY ✦✦✦

PATHS *Byways, stream sides and some field paths, 7 stiles*

LANDSCAPE *Grassy hillsides and valleys*

SUGGESTED MAP *OS Explorer 142 Shepton Mallet*

START / FINISH *Grid reference: ST 739583*

DOG FRIENDLINESS *Mostly pasture*

PARKING *Street parking in village centre, or large car park in Station Road*

PUBLIC TOILETS *None en route*

When you walk through this quiet corner of Somerset, it certainly doesn't strike you as an industrial landscape. As you climb out of the Wellow Valley you might notice some odd conical hills. And then, at Combe Hay, with its lovely medieval manor house, there is some very peculiar 18th-century brickwork. Combe Hay and Wellow were actually at the heart of Somerset's industrial revolution. And the last coal mine here only closed in the 1970s.

Roman Coal Field

Like so much in Somerset, it started with the Romans. In the Temple of Minerva in nearby Bath, a fire burned – according to some historians, a living coal fire. Certainly by the 16th century the mines were going down. Squashed between the Mendips and the Cotswolds, the Somerset coal field is small and awkward. Many of the veins are vertical, and only a few feet (a metre or so) in width. So coal might be hacked from overhead, on an improvised platform jammed across a narrow shaft. And always, for miner and mine owner alike, there was the threat of cheaper and easier coal coming up the River Avon from Wales.

This brings us to the engineering bricks in the field at Combe Hay. To move 100,000 tons of coal a year to Bath a canal was constructed that was ambitious even by the standards of the enterprising 18th century. Over its length of just 10 miles (16.1km), from Paulton Basin to Bath, the Somersetshire Coal Canal had two aqueducts and a tunnel. Furthermore, there was the problem of the 165ft (50m) climb on to Combe Hay Hill. The solution was, in effect, an underwater elevator. A barge on the upper canal entered a floating metal box called a caisson. The caisson was sealed, and water pumped in until it started to sink. It sank for 50ft (15m) to the bottom of the shaft. Its door was then matched up to a door in the base of the shaft; both doors were opened; and the barge floated out. The process would take seven minutes, unless the caisson got stuck. The ground around the caisson shaft is fuller's earth, which expands when wetted, and this may have caused the sides of the shaft to bulge inwards. The caissons

WELLOW

were abandoned after only two years and replaced with an inclined plane. The southern branch of the canal, through Wellow to Radstock, was never completed. Instead, a horse-drawn tramway carried the coal out. Both canal and tramway were replaced by the railway, which in its turn has been superseded by motor roads.

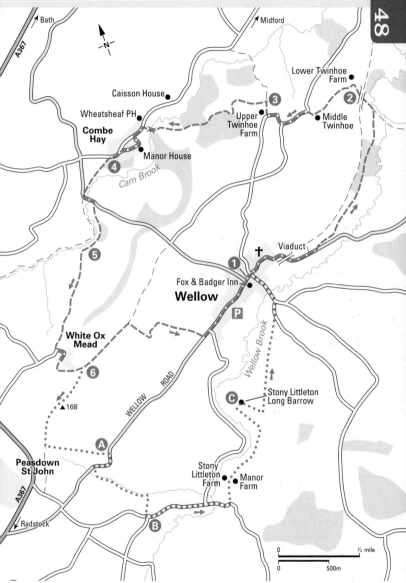

WALK 48 DIRECTIONS

❶ Head out past the church and under a viaduct. Soon after Wellow Trekking a track starts just above the road. Where it becomes unclear, keep going, to the hedge ahead. The track continues above it, and runs down through a soggy wood, then down to the valley floor. It then turns up left to pass under a railway bridge.

2 Just before Lower Twinhoe Farm turn left into a signposted green track. At the hilltop the track fades into a field. Bear right, before Middle Twinhoe, to a small gate and then a larger one. Turn right along the farm's driveway to a lane. Turn left, then down right around farm buildings, and bend left towards Upper Twinhoe. Just before this farm a signed track descends to the right.

> ### WHERE TO EAT AND DRINK
>
> The Fox and Badger is at the walk's start. It is an old pub with food, beer and skittles and specialises in inserting fine local cheeses into its ploughman's lunch. Dogs welcome, on leads. The Wheatsheaf at Combe Hay serves real ales and good food (closed Mondays).

3 After 130yds (119m) turn left through a bridleway gate and along a field top. The path then slants down through scrubby woodland towards Combe Hay. From the wood edge follow the lower edge of a field to a stone bridge into the village. Follow the main lane left, to pass the Manor House.

4 After the last house of Combe Hay, find a gap in the wall on the left. Fork right, down to the Cam Brook, and follow it to a road bridge (Combe Hay Bridge).

> ### WHILE YOU'RE THERE
>
> Radstock Museum gives much of its space to the coal industry. It has a reconstructed mine tunnel and items from that most attractive of ages (to look at afterwards if not to live through), the industrial 18th century.

Cross it and continue with the stream down on your right through a field and a wood. Follow the stream along another field to a stile, then along the foot of a short field to a hedge gap.

5 Don't go through this hedge gap, but turn left up the field-edge to a stile on the right instead. Slant up across the next field to its far top corner and a nettly way between high thorns. At the top of this bear right in a rutted track to a lane. Turn uphill to White Ox Mead, and follow the lane to the right for another 60yds (55m) to a kissing gate on the right. Slant up to a field gate and a stile, and turn up a tarred track to where it divides near a shed without walls.

6 Keep ahead on a track along the hill crest. Ignore a waymarked stile to pass under high- and low-voltage electric cables. Here a small metal gate on the right leads to a hoof-printed path down beside a fence. At the foot of the field turn left, then left again (uphill), round a corner to a gate. Turn left across the field top and down its edge to the street leading into Wellow.

> ### WHAT TO LOOK OUT FOR
>
> In all but the driest of conditions, the descent towards Combe Hay features some of the stickiest mud anywhere. The reason is fuller's earth: this is the special sort of clay (aluminium silicate) that was mined and used to wash wool with – as well as grease, it also absorbs water. The consequent swelling is what caused the caisson shaft at Combe Hay to bulge inwards and jam.

Wellow Brook and Stony Littleton Long Barrow

Extend your walk to a magnificently restored ancient burial feature.

See map and information panel for Walk 48

DISTANCE 9 miles (14.5km) **MINIMUM TIME** 4hrs 45min
ASCENT/GRADIENT 900ft (274m) ▲▲▲ **LEVEL OF DIFFICULTY** +++
NOTE A torch is useful in the long barrow

WALK 49 DIRECTIONS
(Walk 48 option)

At Point **6** of Walk 48 turn right above the shed without walls. The track becomes narrower between overgrown banks as it descends into the valley of the Wellow Brook. Where it reaches a gate, turn left into a hedged path that becomes a wide, muddy track to reach Wellow Road, Point **A**.

Turn right along the lane as it dips to a bridge. Here turn left through two grey gates into a tractor graveyard. Bear right to cross the stream, and head down alongside it over three stiles. Cross a stony, sunken track to another stile; continue downstream, through two more fields, until a track leads up to the right to join a lane, Point **B**.

Turn left, downhill, to cross a bridge over the Wellow Brook. After 130yds (119m) turn left into a track, with sign 'Manor Farm'. This passes below the fine manor house and above Stony Littleton Farm into a rougher track. This wanders down to a gate with bridleway signpost. Turn left, to ascend with a hedge on your left to join a green track. Before the top of this turn left over a stile signposted for the Long

Barrow. Follow the field top until two more stiles lead up to Stony Littleton Long Barrow (Point **C**).

Built in the New Stone Age (about 5,000 years ago), the long barrow has a low, stone entrance at its southern end, leading to a passage with grave chambers on either side. A fossil ammonite is displayed at the entrance. The roof has been recently repaired by English Heritage – the damage was started by a farmer in 1760 seeking stone for track repairs. The interior should now be safe; but even so it would be wise to leave one member of the party outside.

Return down over one stile, then turn left towards a gate on the previous track. Don't go through, but turn left alongside the hedge. From the hedge end, contour onwards to a gate with a hedged track beyond. Where this reaches a lane, turn down left. The road crosses a ford, with a stone footbridge alongside, then rises into Wellow.

Bath's Therapeutic Waters

Where the Romans rested: by canal and by river around Regency Bath.

DISTANCE	4 miles (6.4km)
MINIMUM TIME	1hr 40min
ASCENT/GRADIENT	200ft (60m) ▲▲▲
LEVEL OF DIFFICULTY	✦✦✦
PATHS	Surfaced paths and streets, no stiles
LANDSCAPE	Canal and riverside, and England's most handsome town
SUGGESTED MAP	OS Explorer 155 Bristol & Bath
START / FINISH	Grid reference: ST 758649
DOG FRIENDLINESS	Urban walk – dogs on leads (fines for fouling)
PARKING	Street parking on Sydney Wharf or use the park & ride
PUBLIC TOILETS	At Victoria Park, and behind Holburne Museum

WALK 50 DIRECTIONS

Start where the Kennet and Avon Canal passes under Bathwick Hill. At a small Tesco, steps lead down to the tow path. Turn right (with canal on left and town centre down to the right), passing moored narrowboats. After two sets of locks the tow path ends at the low bridge of the A36 (Pulteney Road).

Cross the lock gate in front of this road bridge and go down some steps to an underpass. Follow the canal under two bridges to turn left alongside the River Avon. Pass under the railway and then climb to a concrete footbridge. Cross the dual-carriageway, Churchill Bridge just beyond, and continue on Avon Walkway, now with the river on your left.

Follow the path under the girders of the Midland Bridge, the covered bridge known as the 'Sainsbury-Homebase', and a suspension footbridge. Then turn up right, just before a girder footbridge. Turn away from this bridge, to the busy Midland Road.

Cross and turn left alongside Victoria Park to a gate at its corner. Pass through a play area. Toilets are ahead; otherwise turn uphill on steps and paved paths and into the botanic garden.

Bear left and follow any of a multitude of paths to a pond. Pass round this to the very top of the gardens, near the Minerva Temple.

The centre of the Earth is hot because its low-level radioactivity generates energy that has no way to escape. Surface water that trickles far enough down gets heated. Hot water rises, so it then starts to trickle back up again. Sometimes it gets right